— ART THERAPY —
WITH FAMILIES
IN CRISIS
Overcoming Resistance
Through Nonverbal Expression

–ART THERAPY–
WITH FAMILIES
IN CRISIS

*Overcoming Resistance
Through Nonverbal Expression*

EDITED BY

DEBRA LINESCH, Ph.D.

BRUNNER/MAZEL *Publishers* • NEW YORK

Library of Congress Cataloging-in-Publication Data
Art therapy with families in crisis : overcoming resistance through
  nonverbal expression / edited by Debra Linesch.
      p.   cm.
  Includes bibliographical references and index.
  ISBN 0-87630-638-5
  1. Art therapy.   2. Family psychotherapy.   I. Linesch, Debra
Greenspoon
RC489.A7A79   1993
616.89′156—dc20   92-27839
                                                                CIP

Published by
BRUNNER/MAZEL, INC.
19 Union Square West
New York, New York 10003

Manufactured in the United States of America

10   9   8   7   6   5   4   3   2   1

Contents

Introduction

This book addresses the potentially profound connections between the process of making art and the experience of family therapy. To do so, it formulates three questions about the relationship between the creative process and the needs of particularly dysfunctional families. It attempts to explain, through illustration rather than definition, the extraordinary opportunity made available to the family by the art process.

Family therapy has become an important modality in working with the casualties and victims of today's chaotic world. For many years art therapists (Kwiatkowska, 1978; Landgarten, 1987) have written about the particular approaches to family therapy that can be augmented and supported by the utilization of the art process. Going one step further, it is the intent of this book to focus on the nature of the relationship between the art experience and the curative process as it becomes part of the treatment intervention.

The first chapter of this book begins with a brief exploration of family systems and the creative process as psychotherapy. Based on these explorations, three fundamental questions emerge that provide an opportunity for understanding the psychotherapeutic phenomenon experienced when distressed families encounter the art therapy process.

1. What are the characteristics of the special needs families discussed in this book that invite the implementation of an art therapy process?
2. What are the characteristics of the art process that seem responsive to these families' special needs?
3. What is unique about the curative relationship between the needs of these families and the art interventions?

Chapter 1 concludes with a brief attempt to illustrate how the clinical material discussed in subsequent chapters answers these emergent questions. However, it is a thorough reading of the case material in Chapters 2 through 6 that will deepen our understanding of these simply sketched answers.

The final chapter of this book presents a summation of the answers to the questions that emerge in Chapter 1 and are explored through clinical illustration in the case material that followed.

– SECTION I –

ASKING
THE
QUESTIONS

-1-

Family Systems and the Creative Process: The First Look

Debra Linesch

In this chapter, conceptual models are developed to assist the process of focusing the questions that will illuminate the phenomena that occur when distressed family systems encounter the art therapy process.

FOCUSING THE QUESTIONS

The First Question

The first in the series of emerging questions becomes, ''What are the characteristics of special-needs families that invite the implementation of the art process?''

Moving Toward Answers

More than a combination of individuals functioning autonomously, a family is an interactive system of relationships in which each member inextricably affects every other member, as is illustrated in Figure 1.1.

Just as it is the establishment of this interactive pattern that gives the family its idiosyncratic character, it is the investigation of this pattern that helps the clinician to assess difficulties. Different theorists focus on different aspects of this fundamental pattern to conceptualize assessment. For example, Minuchin (1974) emphasizes the boundaries between subsystems (indi-

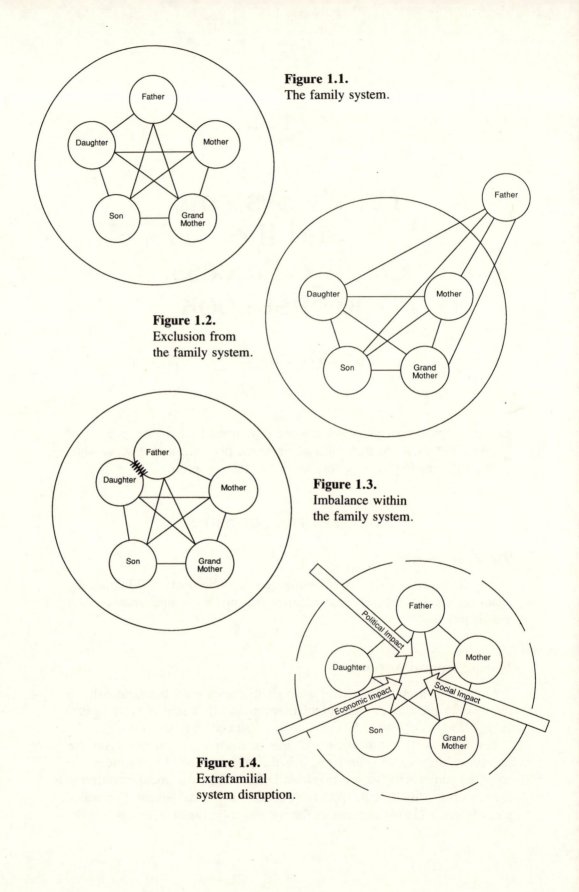

Figure 1.1.
The family system.

Figure 1.2.
Exclusion from
the family system.

Figure 1.3.
Imbalance within
the family system.

Figure 1.4.
Extrafamilial
system disruption.

viduals) in the large system (the family), whereas Satir (1967) focuses on the way in which the family members communicate with one another.

Acknowledging the possibility of complication through oversimplification, I propose, for the purpose of developing a model, a list of three basic disturbances to healthy family functioning. This list attempts to cross boundaries between schools of thought and to synthesize generalized truths about family systems that I have observed in my own clinical work. In creating this list, I hope to avoid identifying with any particular theory and to concentrate on the description of phenomena that frequently appear as pivotal to system disruption. Although every clinical scenario presents as a very complex system, the following hypothetical simplifications create three categories that are useful for conceptualizing family system disruptions. Figure 1.1 will be modified for each inclusion in this list to illustrate the dysfunction.

The first pattern disruption involves the exclusion of one system member. Whether the behavior is self-imposed or system-imposed, this isolation affects the entire system, just as the system affects the isolate. As is suggested in Figure 1.2, the configuration of the system has to readjust to the exclusion and the interrelationships among all members shift in response. In this hypothetical example, as the father is excluded from the family, the interpersonal connections are restructured, tightening between some of the remaining family members and loosening between others. Only one individual has departed, but all the parts of the system have shifted as a result.

The second pattern of dysfunction can be identified as an imbalance in relationship and may involve any grouping of individuals within the system. The intensity of relationship that creates the imbalance may be positive or negative. Figure 1.3 illustrates the manner in which an enmeshed dyad causes the entire system to reconfigure, affecting all the relationships within the family. In this hypothetical example, a strong relationship has intensified between daughter and father. That connection has caused the entire family system to restructure itself as the other family members redefine their interpersonal relationships in terms of this dyadic intensification.

The third pattern of dysfunction involves extrafamilial phenomena that affect the structure of the system. This external experience may be negative or positive. Figure 1.4 illustrates the manner in which social, economic, and political events can shake up the family system and cause its reconfiguration. In this hypothetical example, the family has been severely disrupted by a crisis that has limited their income, disrupted their social status, and ostracized them from their community. The interpersonal relationships between all members of this family are affected by the stress of reconfiguration, and the family is characterized by chaos.

THE CREATIVE PROCESS AND PSYCHOTHERAPY

The Question

In this section, the emergent question becomes, ''What are the characteristics of the art process that seem responsive to these families' special needs?''

Moving Toward Answers

The art process, as described throughout the literature of art therapy, offers a variety of experiences that can promote change. Again, at the risk of oversimplification and based on my own experience as an art therapist, I have categorized these opportunities into three main avenues for facilitating therapeutic growth.

The primary opportunity offered by the art process is for self-expression. The artistic endeavor is an alternative to the predominant modality of communication in our culture and as such stimulates change. As individuals (or families) express themselves in changed ways, the content and usefulness of their expression change also. The art experience provides one with access to primary process and latent unconscious material. It can bypass well-entrenched defenses that have become obstacles to understanding and self-actualization, as illustrated in Figure 1.5.

A second opportunity offered by the art process involves interpersonal communication and relationship building. In psychotherapy, attempts at genuine dialogue between individuals can be aborted by rigid patterns of behavior and ritual. A dependence on words can prevent individuals (and families) from finding the opportunities for invigorating their communication

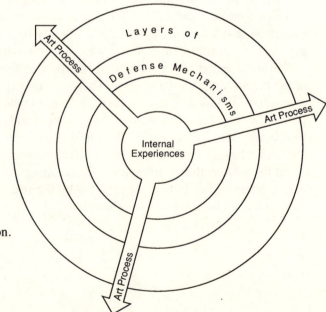

Figure 1.5.
Facilitating self-expression.

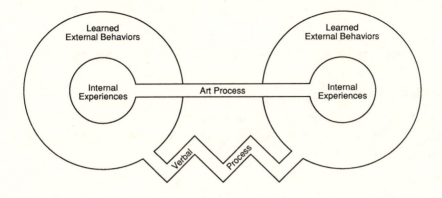

Figure 1.6. Facilitating interpersonal communication.

styles. The art process can offer a means for liberating bound and redundant interpersonal styles that make relationships stale and rigid. Figure 1.6 illustrates the manner in which the art process facilitates genuine communications.

The third way in which the art process offers experiences that can catalyze change is in its facilitation of energy and empowerment. The making of art is by definition a creative and productive endeavor; as such, it promotes a sense of self and of accomplishment. For individuals (and families) entrenched in failure and impotence, the initiating process of creativity can be liberating and constructive. Figure 1.7 suggests a model for understanding the way in which the art process enables the self to become active and to participate. Hopelessness, despair, anxiety, and depression can be counteracted as the self rejuvenates.

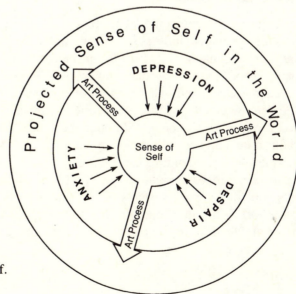

Figure 1.7.
Promoting a sense of self.

DISTRESSED FAMILIES AND THE ART PROCESS

The Question

In this section, the final and most significant question emerges, "What is unique about the curative relationship between the needs of these families and the art interventions?"

Moving Toward Answers

Intuitively, we assume there must be a match between dysfunctional family patterns and the art process with its change-promoting opportunities, and consider the simple models being developed in this chapter in order to theorize about its form. It is tempting to superimpose the graphic models of intrapsychic and interpersonal facilitation (Figures 1.5, 1.6, and 1.7) upon the graphic models of family dysfunction (Figures 1.2, 1.3, and 1.4) and conceptualize the match. However, in an effort to ground what would be a purely hypothetical relationship in observable phenomena, it is my intent to explore the clinical material included in the remainder of this book to develop the possibilities of integration between family needs and art making.

ANSWERS EMERGE FROM CLINICAL MATERIAL

First Clinical Example

Chapter 2 presents a model for family art therapy crisis intervention. As the author/therapist outlines the history and theory of crisis intervention, she illustrates the manner in which the art modality is particularly well suited to the needs of families in situational crises. She explains how the art process affects the chaos and disintegration of families experiencing severe stress. The list she creates of three categories of impact integrates well with the overall theme of this book. Although the author describes two family cases to illustrate a number of art therapy interventions, she is careful to maintain a framework that identifies the following three opportunities provided by the art therapy process: cognition and problem-solving, ventilation of affect, and work with family systems. This case material supports the conceptual framework being developed in this book. Sustaining the specific focus of crisis intervention, it provides us with beginning answers to the three questions articulated earlier.

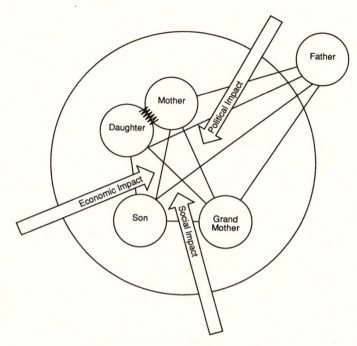

Figure 1.8.
The family in crisis.

Question 1

What are the characteristics of families in crisis that invite the implementation of the art therapy process?

Although crises can occur in many forms, Chapter 2 explains the underlying characteristics that define a family requiring crisis intervention. The author discusses the experience of loss as a crucial element of the crisis state, as well as of the consequent disequilibrium (loss of equilibrium in the family). In an effort to utilize the concepts created earlier, Figure 1.8 has been created to illustrate the kind of overall systemic disintegration that can occur in a major family crisis. In this diagram, as is frequently the case, external elements have intruded upon the weakened family boundaries, members have been excluded from the system, and relationships have taken on characteristics of imbalance.

Question 2

What are the characteristics of the art process that seem responsive to families in crisis?

Figure 1.8 provides a representation of a chaotic family, indicating the characteristics that make it particularly amenable to art therapy intervention. Figure 1.9 illustrates the potential of the art process that will be meaningful to the familial needs represented in Figure 1.8. The diagram illustrates the manner in which the art process fundamentally assists the surfacing of

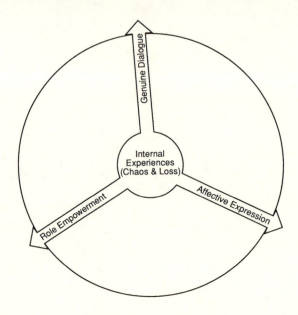

Figure 1.9. The art process: surfacing internal experiences.

internal experiences. With families in crisis, it is most helpful to encourage three facets of this experience. Affective expression can be supported, dialogue and communication can be strengthened, and structural interventions (such as role empowerment) can be achieved through assigned art tasks.

Question 3

What is unique about the curative relationship between the needs of families in crisis and art interventions?

No diagram has been created to illustrate the profound impact of the art process (Figure 1.9) on the family in crisis (Figure 1.8). Efforts to create one result in gross oversimplification and a loss of complexity. It is the clarity and clinical richness of Chapter 2 that will provide the illustration that begins to answer this third and complicated question. Tentative answers, which emerge from the clinical material, will be presented at the conclusion of this book.

Second Clinical Example

The case material presented in Chapter 3 is a richly detailed exploration of the art process with single-parent families. It begins with a comprehensive overview of the dynamics of single-parent families, leaning heavily toward the author/therapist's obvious orientation as a structural family therapist. As she reviews the stresses and problems of the children and (most typically) the mothers in these families, the rationale for structural interventions is fully supported. The chapter provides clinical examples from two different families, illustrating the author/therapist's central idea that the art process facilitates the creation of metaphors that support the interventions that need to be prioritized in work with single-parent families.

As the case material is described, it becomes increasingly clear that the use of imagery and the creative process have great impact on the author/therapist's five goals: to create a safe place, to empower the mother, to firm up the generational boundaries, to reorganize the family structure, and to encourage the expression of feeling. Sustaining the specific focus of structural family therapy with single parents, this case material provides us with additional answers to the three questions articulated earlier.

Question 1

What are the characteristics of single-parent families that invite the implementation of the art therapy process?

Chapter 3 provides a clear understanding of the dynamics of the single-parent family. The author/therapist articulates the experience of loss, the weakening of the family system, and the consequent breakdown in family organization. Figure 1.10 illustrates this phenomenon and helps integrate the clinical material of the chapter into the book's overall framework.

Figure 1.10 illustrates the imbalanced system that is typically a consequence of the shift from two-parent to single-parent households. Children's dependency on the remaining parent is intensified, tremendous anger is experienced in all directions, and the mother is left depleted, alone, and unfamiliar with the expectations and demands of the new role. As such, the family is a system crying out for restructuring and support.

Figure 1.10. The single-parent system.

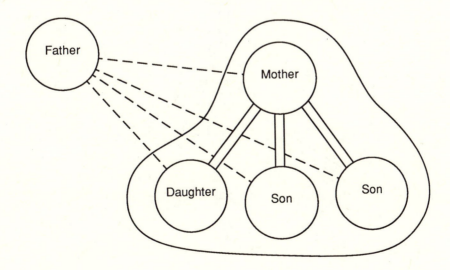

Question 2

What are the characteristics of the art process that seem responsive to single-parent families?

Chapter 3 creates a list of five interventions that are valuable in the treatment of single-parent families. It is not difficult to reorganize these five interventions into the three basic categories used to explain how the art process helps all the families discussed in this book: personal affective expression augmented, interfamilial communication facilitated (through concrete symbolic messages), and changing roles acknowledged and supported. In these ways the art process aids the fundamental task of reorganizing the family structure. The process is illustrated in Figure 1.11.

Question 3

What is unique about the curative relationship between the needs of single-parent families and art interventions?

No diagram has been created to illustrate the profound impact of the art process (Figure 1.11) on the single-parent family (Figure 1.10). It is within the art experiences of the two families so eloquently described in Chapter 3 that the answers to this fundamental question lie. The concluding chapter will attempt to articulate the answers as they emerge from the clinical material.

Figure 1.11.   The art process: exposing internal experiences.

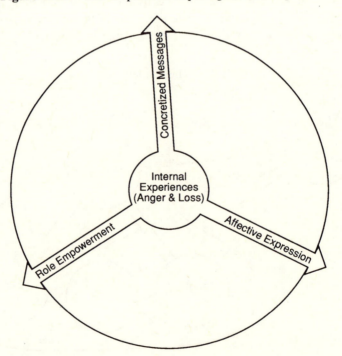

Third Clinical Example

Chapter 4 presents the dynamics of an alcoholic family and the impact made on it by art therapy interventions. The author/therapist begins by outlining the current clinical understanding and treatment approaches with families involved in alcohol abuse. As a result, the following clinical example, in all its richness of detail, is well grounded in an overall dynamic understanding. The chapter illustrates the way in which art therapy exposes pathological family interaction and patterns, thereby offering a foundation for therapeutic intervention. The material provides us with additional answers to the three questions articulated earlier.

Question 1

What are the characteristics of alcoholic families that invite the implementation of the art therapy process?

Although there are many patterns of familial disruption caused by alcohol abuse, the alcoholism typically creates an overall family ambiance that is precarious, full of double messages and confusion. Rigid roles are frequently assigned to family members. These are useful in maintaining homeostasis that colludes with the alcoholic dependency, but are not useful in supporting family or individual psychological health. Roles commonly seen include those of co-dependents, enablers, scapegoats, and heroes.

The description in Chapter 4 of a particular family illustrates the manner in which a family of seven structures itself around the father's alcoholism. Interestingly, as is described in the chapter, the family does not recognize the alcohol abuse as a problem, but enters treatment through its focus on the troubled behavior of the 13-year-old identified patient (i.e., scapegoat). Figure 1.12 illustrates the relationships of collusion and exclusion that characterize the mother's and the children's efforts to deny the psychopathology of substance abuse.

Question 2

What are the characteristics of the art process that seem responsive to alcoholic families?

Figure 1.13 illustrates the potential of the art process that will be meaningful to the extraordinary familial needs represented in Figure 1.12.

Fundamental to work with alcoholic families is the capacity to assess concealed and unconscious material within the family system. The diagram in Figure 1.13 illustrates the manner in which the art process, through the

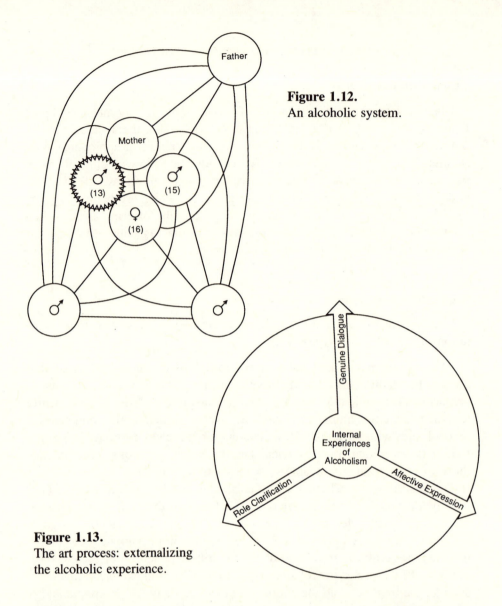

Figure 1.12.
An alcoholic system.

Figure 1.13.
The art process: externalizing
the alcoholic experience.

use of metaphor and visual symbols, has this ability. As individual family members are encouraged, through the use of directives, to express their feelings and genuinely address each other, the created products become vehicles for breaking down the family's walls of denial. Consequently, roles can be clarified and, it is hoped, amended as internal experiences are more clearly recognized and acknowledged.

Question 3

What is unique about the curative relationship between the needs of alcoholic families and art interventions?

No diagram has been created to illustrate the profound impact of the art process (Figure 1.13) on the alcoholic family (Figure 1.12). The illustrative case material of Chapter 4 offers some comprehension of the complex answers to this fundamental third question. The conclusion of this book will offer an articulation of the emergent answers.

Fourth Clinical Example

Chapter 5 presents a family-based model of intervention with victims of incestuous sexual abuse. The author/therapist understands and discusses the roots of the self-perpetuating cycle of abuse within both family and societal systems. Consequently, the model of intervention in the chapter offers concepts and techniques that have an impact on the dynamics that have isolated victims, perpetrators, and family members. Particularly powerful is the discussion of the manner in which the family colludes with the victim's dismissal of the abuse experience. It is the author/therapist's understanding of this core dynamic that permeates the directives and interventions that provide the framework for her model.

The chapter introduces the reader to five young female abuse victims and discusses their participation, along with a nonperpetrating family member, in an 11-session multiple-family art therapy group. The author/therapist describes the sessions in detail, focusing on the three goals that stem from her dynamic understanding: encouraging the child's self-expression, supporting improved parenting efforts, and increasing intergenerational interactions. This case material provides us with additional answers to the three questions articulated earlier.

Question 1

What are the characteristics of families victimized by incestuous sexual abuse that invite implementation of the art therapy process?

The author/therapist discusses the family systems that perpetuate abuse as characterized by the following: inappropriate expression of feelings, erosion of self-trust or self-concept, and lack of appropriate acceptance of responsibility. These characteristics create an environment in which the victims (and family members) dismiss the internal and external experiences around the abuse. An understanding of this phenomenon helps explain the rigidity of response frequently observed in psychotherapy with sexual abuse families. Figure 1.14 attempts to illustrate the chapter's conceptual understanding of this population and to integrate it into the overall framework of this book.

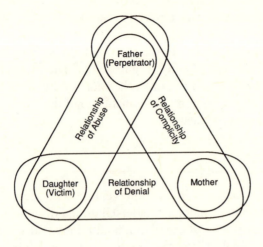

Figure 1.14.
A sexually abusive system.

The diagram in Figure 1.14 graphically conveys the complexities of roles and interpersonal rituals that support the homeostasis and collude with the denial of the sexual abuse family.

Question 2

What are the characteristics of the art process that seem responsive to families victimized by incestuous sexual abuse?

Figure 1.15 illustrates the potential of the art process that will be particularly meaningful to the complex set of needs so powerfully illustrated in Figure 1.14.

The diagram suggests how the art process can liberate the repressed recognition of the abuse experience, facilitate intergenerational acknowledgment, and, in the process, help empower all family members to accept and fulfill role obligations and responsibilities.

Figure 1.15.
The art process: liberating the abusive experience.

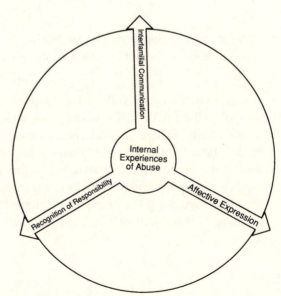

Question 3

What is unique about the curative relationship between the needs of incestuous sexual abuse families and art interventions?

No diagram has been created to illustrate the profound impact of the art process (Figure 1.15) on the sexual abuse family (Figure 1.14). The descriptive model presented in Chapter 5 provides illustrative material from which comprehension of the answers to this complex question can be gained. The answers will be summarized in the concluding chapter of this book.

Final Clinical Example

Chapter 6 offers us an opportunity to understand the value of the art process with families experiencing unparalleled stresses. Families that have been victim to the ravages of political unrest and have become refugees in a foreign culture are provided with art therapy interventions that are outlined and discussed in this chapter. As the artwork is examined and the stories of the participants are graphically illuminated, the power of the art process becomes clear. In effect, the chapter is a testimonial to the value of the creative process in a society where deep political and social injustices are destructive to individuals and families. Like the earlier case examples, the material provides additional answers to the three questions articulated at the beginning of this chapter.

Question 1

What are the characteristics of Central American refugee families that invite the implementation of the art therapy process?

As discussed by the authors/therapists, the refugee families can be characterized as suffering from the psychological effects of the traumas surrounding migration. The diagnoses of refugee neurosis (Williams & Westermeyer, 1986) and post-traumatic stress disorder (revised third edition of the Diagnostic and Statistical Manual of Mental Disorders) are utilized to provide a full picture of the catastrophe of the refugee experience. Predominant in the discussion of these families is the sense of helpless depression, an affective state that continues the cycle of familial destruction caused by the events surrounding the migration. Figure 1.16 illustrates the totality of the impact on one of these refugee families. Exclusions, subgroupings, and external intrusions are all part of the chaos.

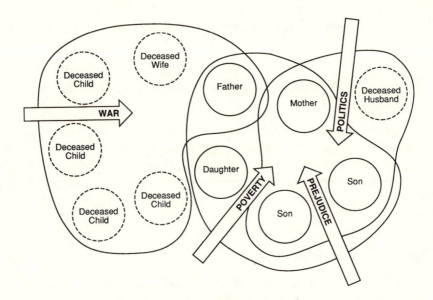

Figure 1.16. A refugee system.

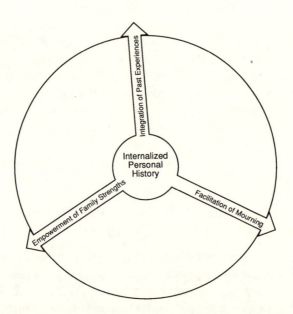

Figure 1.17. The art process: externalizing personal history.

Question 2

What are the characteristics of the art process that seem responsive to Central American refugee families?

Figure 1.17 illustrates ways in which the art process, as discussed in this chapter, seems to offer these families what the authors/therapists describe as "a gesture of healing." The diagram reframes the issues of the chapter within the framework being established throughout this text. The experiences of the refugee participants, although discussed more poetically by the authors/therapists, can be understood in terms of the three questions articulated earlier in the chapter.

When the authors/therapists discuss the manner in which the art experiences facilitate grief and mourning, they are alluding to its power to disencumber affective expression from its defensive obstacles. When they discuss the way in which the symbolic process helps to integrate past experiences within a present reality, they are alluding to the power of the art to facilitate genuine communication. When they discuss the way in which the art process draws out the family's strength from its culture of origin and empowers the family, they are alluding to its power to rejuvenate individuals and enable them to improve their interpersonal functioning. In all three ways, the art process can be understood to offer healing potential to these difficult-to-reach traumatized families.

Question 3

What is unique about the curative relationship between the needs of refugee families and art interventions?

Chapter 6 describes the curative process undertaken by the participants in a multifamily art therapy group for Central American refugees. It is only from the exploration of the imagery and the process that the answers to this third question can begin to emerge. As has been the case in previous chapters, the sequential questioning is intended to more clearly focus the important issues. The answers lie within the clinical discussion and are summarized in the concluding chapter of this book.

BIBLIOGRAPHY

Goldenberg, H., & Goldenberg, I. (1990). *Counseling Today's Families*. Pacific Grove, CA: Brooks/Cole.

Kwiatkowska, H. (1978). *Family Therapy and Evaluation Through Art*. Springfield, IL: Charles C. Thomas.

Landgarten, L. (1987). *Family Art Psychotherapy*. New York: Brunner/Mazel.

Minuchin, S. (1974). *Families and Family Therapy*. Cambridge, MA: Harvard University Press.

Nichols, M. (1987). *The Self in the System*. New York: Brunner/Mazel.

Piercy, F., & Sprenkle, D. (1986). *Family Therapy Sourcebook*. New York: Guilford Press.

Satir, V. (1967). *Conjoint Family Therapy*. Palo Alto, CA: Science and Behavior Books.

Williams, C., & Westermeyer, J. (Eds.). (1986). *Refugee Mental Health in Resettlement Countries*, Washington. DC: Hemisphere.

— SECTION II —

SEARCHING
FOR
ANSWERS

—2—

A Crisis
Intervention Model
for Family Art Therapy

Julie Belnick

The extraordinary versatility of art therapy has allowed for its application in a wide range of therapeutic settings with vastly differing populations. The intrinsic qualities of this modality, such as its ability both to provide structure and to promote free expression, can be drawn upon to meet the varied needs of clients and treatment approaches.

In my work with families in crisis at the Benjamin Rush Center (BRC) in Los Angeles, I recognized what appeared to be a theoretical connection between art therapy and the fundamental concerns of the BRC family crisis intervention model. It was striking to observe how art therapy seemed to enhance the attainment of specific objectives involving cognition and problem-solving, the ventilation of affect, and work with family systems.

Spurred to investigate this dynamic in greater depth, I found that although art therapy had been shown to be a valuable component of various crisis intervention strategies, little had been published about its use in family crises. The few reported cases involved work with one family or at most two families, each following a different treatment format. This inconsistency made it difficult to assess the value of art therapy in facilitating family crisis resolution.

Since the BRC crisis intervention model comprises a clearly defined sequence of steps, one could achieve consistency in evaluating the use of art therapy by following the progress of several families through the treatment process. I proceeded to investigate how art therapy could promote family crisis resolution by facilitating the essential steps of the BRC model.

HISTORY OF CRISIS INTERVENTION

As the stressors in contemporary urban life continue to increase, so do the conditions for crises of all kinds. Families are being faced with dilemmas that overtax their usual coping strategies and thus push them into a state of crisis. It took some time for the mental health field to recognize the unique needs of people in crisis. Once they were recognized, the urgency for developing specialized treatment was realized as well. Lindemann's (1944) seminal study on bereavement was instrumental in bringing about this awareness. As a result of his work, a state of crisis was redefined as a normal response to overwhelming loss. Furthermore, it was noted that people would achieve crisis resolution, adaptively or maladaptively, within four to six weeks of the crisis precipitant.

It followed that ready access to mental health services, as well as a brief treatment approach, was essential to effective intervention. Traditional psychoanalytic treatment was costly, time-consuming, and ill-suited to the specific demands of crisis intervention. Additionally, psychoanalysis was particularly inaccessible to groups of lower socioeconomic status, whereas crisis intervention invited realistic participation of all segments of the community. This awareness, along with the recognition of crisis intervention as an effective treatment modality, culminated in the passage of the Community Mental Health Centers Act of 1963, which established emergency services as one of five primary programs.

Until the 1960s, crisis intervention programs were aimed primarily at treating individuals. With the establishment of family therapy as a treatment modality, programs were developed specifically for families in crisis—where the basic tenets of crisis intervention were found to be equally applicable. For example, the crisis intervention model developed and implemented at BRC began as a model for individuals and grew to encompass work with families.

CRISIS THEORY AND THE EQUILIBRIUM MODEL

The theoretical core of the equilibrium model of crisis intervention (the foundation of the BRC approach) is based on the idea that a state of crisis is a *normal* response to overwhelming loss, resulting in an individual's (or family's) being thrown into psychological disequilibrium. The extent of loss is based on the *subjective perception* of an event as a threat to needs, safety, or meaningful existence. Loss of self-esteem, of sexual-role mastery, or of nurturing can be major crisis precipitants (Strickler & La Sor, 1970).

Family crises parallel individual crises in that a family is propelled into a crisis state when habitual coping is inadequate to maintain the family's equilibrium. Consider the basic premise of family therapy, which states that the family constitutes a system wherein all parts affect the whole. It follows that a family can be thrown into a state of disequilibrium in response to loss affecting one or more members.

The equilibrium model of crisis intervention seeks to return a person (or family) to the precrisis equilibrium—or better. The basic premise that psychic equilibrium will be restored within six weeks lends theoretical structure to the intervention process in that there is a definite time limit on the length of treatment (up to six visits) and precise steps to follow in the intervention process. This supports the necessity for an active stance to be taken by the intervenor. The client is continually directed toward his or her personal coping resources; any dependency on the therapist is discouraged.

STEPS IN THE INTERVENTION PROCESS

Family crisis intervention at BRC is an extension and elaboration of individual crisis intervention techniques, which are examined in the following discussion.

The essential first step in crisis intervention is to assess whether or not the consultee can be treated safely on an outpatient basis. The next task is to identify the precipitating event, which helps differentiate crisis issues from long-term pathology. Often, the consultee is not conscious of exactly what provoked his or her distress. It is helpful to explore the "last contact" (the last interpersonal contact prior to seeking help) because it is almost invariably related symbolically to the core of the crisis. Working backwards chronologically, one can incorporate events leading up to the "last contact" into a time-line, which can facilitate understanding the interrelationship of these events. One can often ascertain how a family has coped in the interim between the crisis precipitant and the decision to finally ask for professional assistance. When the precipitating event has been identified (usually it has occurred a month or less before treatment is sought), one must then uncover the meaning of the event in terms of the threat that it poses to vital psychological needs. It is also important to explore the coping mechanisms usually employed in response to similar threats and the new conditions that have rendered them ineffective.

The consultant condenses the information gleaned thus far into a crisis formulation that is conveyed to the consultee in order to clarify the crisis dynamics. The intent is to provide the consultee with a cognitive grasp of his or her experience, thus opening the way for adaptive coping to emerge.

The development of new coping then becomes a primary focus of treatment. Emotional aspects are addressed throughout the crisis intervention, as the consultant assists the consultee in identifying and expressing underlying feelings. Anticipatory planning review of gains makes up the last phase of intervention.

When one is working with families, the sequential steps of crisis intervention are consistent with those just described. However, they increase in complexity as the practitioner necessarily develops ideas on both individual and family levels.

ART THERAPY AND CRISIS INTERVENTION

Art therapy is uniquely suited to promoting basic goals of crisis intervention involving cognition and problem-solving, ventilation of affect, and work with family systems.

Cognition and Problem-Solving

Attaining cognitive understanding of crisis dynamics is seen as a vital step toward regaining psychic equilibrium. Art therapy provides an individual the opportunity to step back and evaluate the meaning of his or her subjective art expressions. This promotes a person's ability to symbolize, to think, and to think about thinking—processes that are emphasized in cognitive therapy.

Another basic premise of cognitive therapy is the idea that perception is an active process and that each person's view of the world is unique. It follows that a person, although free to choose between alternatives in the environment, is limited by his or her perception. The art experience can facilitate a person's process of choice (or problem-solving) by providing a safe context in which to discover and test out various options.

Visual representation offers a means to express multiple layers of meaning in a condensed format. This aspect of the art experience is strikingly helpful in crisis intervention, where it is essential to uncover the meaning of events. It provides an avenue of exploration that is in marked contrast with verbal representation, which is organized serially in terms of cause and effect.

Cognition and problem-solving are also enhanced by behavioral characteristics of the art experience. The art activity demands problem-solving choices in that the client must weigh alternatives, criticize, and follow through on decisions. Additionally, the graphic product is durable, allowing a client to review and respond to what has been expressed, whereas mental images can fade and evade reevaluation.

Ventilation of Affect

Various theorists and practitioners have addressed the potent capability of art therapy to heighten the subjective experience of affect. Horowitz (1971) notes that the visual modality can help bypass defense mechanisms (such as intellectualization and suppression) that can block affect. Wadeson (1980) reports that art objects can allow people the necessary psychic distance from which to recognize the existence of feelings. From that point, individuals can begin to own and integrate these affects as part of themselves. Additionally, the physical experience of manipulating media (such as squeezing or pounding plasticene), can provide a cathartic release of feelings.

Work with Family Systems

Art therapy can be utilized to illuminate family systems, another vital component of family crisis intervention. A family system can be examined by observation of the family working as a unit on a joint art project: "The value of the art task is threefold: the *process* as a diagnostic, interactional, and rehearsal tool; the *contents* as a means of portraying unconscious and conscious communication; and the *product* as lasting evidence of the group's dynamics" (Landgarten, 1987, p. 5).

It follows that one can also use the art process as a structural intervention by directing the family to work on art tasks in subgroups. For example, in a mother + child + father triad in which the child is triangulated, the parents may be asked to work together while the child remains free to work on his or her own.

FAMILY ART THERAPY CRISIS INTERVENTION MODEL

Art interventions were designed to promote the sequential goals of the BRC treatment model, which are delineated as follows: (1) cognitive understanding of crisis dynamics; (2) identification and expression of crisis-related affect; (3) exploration of previous coping mechanisms and facilitation of adaptive coping through problem-solving; (4) anticipatory planning; (5) summary of gains made during the intervention process.

It is interesting to note that an art intervention directed toward one goal may well provide access to other goals. The *process* of creating the artwork, the *content* of the artwork, and the *interchange* stimulated by the art activity are all vital aspects of the interventions.

ART INTERVENTIONS

Cognitive Understanding of Crisis Dynamics

Assisting people to explore the events culminating in their request for professional help can lead to clarification of crisis dynamics. One might ask members of a family to draw these events and to include what happened the day and the hour before they contacted the clinic. It can be particularly illuminating to have people draw or choose magazine images about the "last contact" (the last interpersonal contact prior to asking for help), since this interaction almost always contains a key to uncovering crisis dynamics. Comparing perceptions of the family before and after the crisis precipitant can provide striking access to underlying crisis dynamics. This can be done with two-dimensional media (e.g., draw your family before and after) or with three-dimensional media such as plasticene, which can facilitate reenactment. For example, one might ask family members to create plasticene images of themselves in order to stage before and after family scenes.

Identification and Expression of Crisis-Related Affect

The metaphorical aspects of magazine collage images often uncover levels of feeling that people are not consciously aware of. Therefore, it can be very useful to ask family members to choose pictures that describe how they feel about the crisis.

Another way to access crisis-related affect is to facilitate the exploration of self-perceptions. To do this, the therapist can ask family members to draw themselves as they feel inside and to draw themselves as they imagine they look to their family.

The use of media can also promote the expression of feeling. For example, the physical act of pounding clay or tearing paper (within safe boundaries) can provide cathartic release of tension.

Exploration of Previous Coping Mechanisms and Facilitation of Adaptive Coping Through Problem-Solving

Asking a family to draw together about how they coped with a similar situation in the past can reinforce strengths and lead to a discussion about why current coping is not meeting their needs. Magazine collage imagery can assist the family to identify why this crisis has rendered their habitual coping ineffective.

To facilitate adaptive coping, the therapist might ask family members to choose pictures or draw images that describe different possible solutions to the problem. Identifying similarities and differences in their works can promote problem-solving. Family members can also be asked to represent themselves and their family as they are now and as they would like to be in the future. This can illuminate individual needs and spark family problem-solving.

Anticipatory Planning

To reinforce adaptive coping, it is important to assist the family to antici-pate events that could disturb their equilibrium and to "rehearse" new coping. The therapist might ask family members to choose magazine pictures that represent their worst fears for the family. They could then draw pictures showing how they would cope with these situations. The family could also be instructed to invent a similar crisis for the future. After discussing how they would cope with the situation, they could concretize their solution by drawing or collaging together.

It is common for families in crisis to be facing upcoming events that are real threats to their equilibrium. In these instances, it is useful to tailor art interventions to a family's specific situation.

Summary of Gains Made During the Intervention Process

An effective way to explore gains is to ask family members to portray themselves and their family at the beginning of treatment and again at the end of treatment. Family members could work together or individually, choosing the media they feel would best express their feelings.

Another way to reinforce gains is to have the family review all of their artwork, since the artwork provides a graphic record of the treatment process.

It is also useful to design an art intervention that highlights and exercises new coping skills. For example, a parent who has been empowered in his or her parenting role could be asked to direct and contain the children within an art task. These kinds of art interventions can provide a springboard for reviewing growth the family experienced in treatment.

CASE STUDIES

The remainder of this chapter will provide case material from two families to illustrate the application of art therapy to the family crisis intervention model. Since single art interventions often provided access to several goals, it was unnecessary to employ art interventions from every category as delineated above. And, as is always the case in responding to real people, the needs of each family dictated which art interventions became the focus of treatment.

THE Z FAMILY

Case History

Emilia, a woman in her 20s and two months pregnant, arrived at BRC with her eight-year-old daughter, Della, and her four-year-old son, Tim.

Emilia had been abused physically and emotionally by her husband throughout their marriage. The crisis precipitant occurred three weeks prior to treatment, when Mr. Z had attacked Emilia physically in the presence of the children, threatening the life of her unborn child. Della was able to dial 911, while Tim tried in vain to pull his dad away from his mom. Emilia credits Della with saving her life, as the police arrived in answer to her call and arrested Mr. Z.

During the next weeks, Emilia coped by asserting herself (taking legal action against her husband). The last contact occurred five minutes before Emilia called BRC. Her lawyer (a middle-aged man) tried to convince her to agree to visitation of the children by their father. During his call, Emilia experienced a feeling of déjà vu, one of being assaulted again by her husband as her lawyer pressured her to do something against her will. The children, meanwhile, overheard her conversation and began to plead with her not to force them to see their father. Emilia decided to call BRC rather than submit to her lawyer's wishes.

Crisis Formulation

The crisis was formulated for Emilia and the children individually, as well as for the family as a unit. For Emilia, the last contact recapitulated the crisis precipitant in that her lawyer was pushing her (as her husband had) to endanger her children. Paralyzed by her ambivalence about assuming an adult role, the cries of her children finally enabled her to defy her lawyer. Emilia experienced a loss of self-esteem and a loss of nurturing (she could no longer depend on her husband), as well as a threat to her sex-role mastery (ability to function as a parent). Past coping (submission) no longer worked, as Emilia could not tolerate risk to her unborn child, who symbolized a choice for life. The crux of Emilia's crisis was formulated as her ambivalence about shifting from a child's role to that of an effective parent.

The children's individual crises were formulated as their weakened tolerance for continuing in their parentified roles, coupled with their ambivalence about relinquishing those roles in the face of Emilia's wavering ability to protect them.

The three individual crises intertwined as part of the systemic crisis of the family renegotiating its hierarchal structure.

Art Therapy and Treatment

Cognitive understanding of crisis dynamics

Figure 2.1 juxtaposes details from collages done by the Z family during their second session. I had asked them to each choose two pictures describing how they felt during the last contact (Emilia's talk with her lawyer about visitation). Emilia identified herself as "one of the kids" as she examined the trapped and vulnerable child in her collage (left, Figure 2.1). This visual identification with the child helped Emilia connect her affective state to her

Figure 2.1.   The Z family's feelings about the "last contact."

TRAPPED
VULNERABLE

disappointed

core struggle of child versus adult roles, giving her a cognitive grasp of her crisis. With the insight that she had functioned as a dependent child relying on her children for nurturance and protection, Emilia was more open to recognizing her children's dilemma.

Della expressed disappointment in her mother's passivity (right, Figure 2.1), and anxiety about her parentified role (note the adult figure attempting to control the enormous dinosaur). Tim spontaneously reached for the image of a dead mother and child (top, Figure 2.1), only to discard it later in favor of a benign picture. Although the picture was too confrontive for Tim to tolerate, he had revealed his mortal terror at having experienced the loss of his mother's protection. It became clear that it was increasingly difficult for him to function in his parentified role and that he needed his mother to assume control.

Identification and expression of crisis-related affect

In the discussion of Figure 2.1 in the previous section, it is apparent that cognitive understanding evolved through the family's identification and expression of affect. More important, the art intervention allowed the four-year-old the means to communicate his feelings without words.

Figure 2.2 reveals how the *process* of working with art media provided Tim additional opportunities to identify and express feelings. In their third session, I asked the Z family to each sculpt a plasticene self-image and to use these to reenact scenes from family life before and after the crisis.

Significantly, Tim made an image of his mother instead of himself. Then, he made a figure of his father and proceeded to destroy him, as you can see by the pile of body parts to the left of the figure in Figure 2.2. The art material gave this child an opportunity to vent his rage in a physical and concrete manner. Tim pounded and mutilated his father's image repeatedly in a cathartic attempt to gain a sense of mastery over the aggressor. This episode also replayed the crisis dynamics, as Tim, in his role as parentified child, acted out his fantasy of protecting his mother.

This same art intervention assisted in the expression of affect in another way, as Della asked her mother for help in constructing her plasticene self-image (right, Figure 2.3). When Emilia refused to help, as she was preoccupied with her own sculpture, Della became angry and despondent. Della was helped to communicate her feelings to her mom, who was able to gain awareness of how much her daughter needed to depend on her. Emilia was faced with another painful recognition of her ambivalence about mothering. Once again, the expression of affect reinforced cognitive understanding.

Figure 2.2. Catharsis for Tim.

Figure 2.3. Emilia and Della develop self-images.

Exploration of previous coping mechanisms and facilitation of adaptive coping through problem-solving

In their fourth session, Della and Tim were asked to depict what it is like to be a child and what it is like to be a parent. This intervention was aimed at exploring their ambivalence about shifting roles in the family. It also encompassed an inquiry into past and present coping.

Notice the image in the upper left of Della's collage (Figure 2.4). She identified herself as the parent (doctor) of her mother, the helpless infant. When asked what would happen if this parent went away, she responded that the baby would die. Hearing this, Emilia interjected that the baby would cry, but would help itself when it realized it was alone. She proceeded to reassure her daughter that she would survive and succeed in her new role as parent. In this instance, the art clearly exposed Della's fear of losing her mother entirely if she let go of her parentified role. Affected by the graphic imagery and related associations, Emilia was spurred to engage as a parent

Figure 2.4. Della's ambivalence about shifting roles.

Say this is me. Mom is the kid I am the parent.

This is me at eight years old having fun at somewhere.

Figure 2.5. Tim tries to fill his father's shoes.

with Della. Thus, past and present coping were illuminated through the art intervention.

Figure 2.5 shows a detail from Tim's collage, illustrating his perception of being a child. Notice the young boy tying the laces of an enormous shoe. When asked whose shoe this might be, Tim identified it as belonging to his father. This led to a discussion about how Tim's childhood experience was dominated by his attempts to fill his father's shoes. Observe how the image of a dream-couple covers most of the shoe. Tim added this image as we spoke, revealing his wish for parents who could relieve him of his burden. His struggle with past and present coping was made evident in his artwork.

Anticipatory planning

Two upcoming events provided the Z family important material for anticipatory planning—termination of treatment (the next session would be their last of six) and a court hearing to determine visitation guidelines with Mr. Z.

First, the family was asked to draw about how they would feel after saying goodbye to this therapist. Their drawings revealed both sadness and hope about the future. Emilia was able to recognize that part of her sadness embodied a fear of losing support and having to rely on her own strength. Anticipating this loss helped Emilia address her own fears and acknowledge her children's similar insecurities. She was empowered to reassure them that she would remain as their protector.

Me older than my age—playing ball with my brother.

by:

Figure 2.6. Struggling with a parentified role.

A similar dynamic emerged in exploring feelings about the court hearing, in which the children would be facing their father. Tim became agitated and drew a fantasy in which he rescued his mother and sister from Mr. Z by flying them off in a spaceship. He finished his drawing by tearing the paper into bits. Tim's anticipatory drawing strongly resembled the original crisis precipitant in which he tried in vain to vanquish his father.

Emilia was able to see her son's struggle and intervene by stating that she would take responsibility for protecting him and his sister. Anticipatory planning became a vehicle for rehearsing new coping, catalyzed by the emotions graphically revealed in the Z family's artwork.

Summary of gains

At the beginning of their last session, Della drew spontaneously (Figure 2.6), providing the family with a potent review of treatment. She began by carefully rendering the stiff, stylized girl/woman with hands upheld and empty, and commented that this was a picture of herself. When asked how old the figure appeared to be, she replied that it was her age (eight), while Emilia commented that the figure looked more like herself (late twenties). Della was able to see her struggle with parentification reflected in her drawing. When I asked what the figure was reaching for, Della then added the ball and said that she wanted to play, revealing her desire to embody the child.

The last art intervention requested that Emilia assume a leadership role and direct the children in the creation of a family drawing (Figure 2.7). Emilia's landscape filled the left half, while the children shared the remainder of the page, mirroring this mother's progress toward assuming an adult role with her children.

Della's girl/woman and the family drawing poignantly summarized the family's experience in treatment. In six weeks they had reached a new, yet fragile equilibrium. They had negotiated a shift toward a new family structure—one in which Emilia began to assert herself as a mother along with one in which the children cautiously began to look to her for protection. Art therapy had provided them unique access to understanding the meaning of their crisis; to identifying and expressing their feelings; to recognizing their past coping and engaging in new ways of relating to each other.

Figure 2.7.   Emilia is empowered.

The J Family

Case History

Lou, a man in his late 30s, arrived at the clinic with Eve, his 12-year-old daughter. A brief history revealed that Lou and his wife had divorced when Eve was three years old, with Eve's mother retaining custody. The mother remarried five years later (Eve expressed fear and hatred of her stepfather), while Lou maintained visitation with Eve throughout. Five months prior to treatment, Eve's mother had agreed to let Eve live with Lou, as Eve's relationship with her stepfather was becoming increasingly tumultuous. Eve functioned well in her father's home until one month prior to treatment, when she began refusing to attend school, claiming that her peers were mean to her. She remained truant, completing her school work at home.

The crisis precipitant occurred five days prior to treatment, when Lou and his ex-wife decided to work as a parental team to insist on Eve's return to school. Eve's mother came to Lou's home and the two parents confronted their daughter, provoking angry resistance.

During the interim before treatment, Eve coped by provoking a series of chaotic shifts in the family system (in an unconscious effort to resolve long-term family issues): a minor suicide attempt the day after the crisis precipitant once again elicited the mother's presence and prompted the parental decision that Eve return to live with her mother. Lou coped by relinquishing responsibility for Eve to his ex-wife.

Lou made the decision to come to the clinic after a telephone conversation with his ex-wife (the last contact) in which it was determined that Eve should once again return to live with him—two days after she had moved back with her mother. Eve had provoked this decision by fighting with her stepfather.

Crisis Formulation

The decision to have Eve return to her father's home contradicted Lou's usual coping response—to relinquish responsibility. He was again confronted with his feelings of failure as a parent and with his ambivalence about how to involve himself with his family. On an essential level, Lou's crisis was based on his fear of taking control of his life.

Eve's crisis was formulated as her unsuccessful quest to find a home in which she could feel settled and secure. Her attempts to reshape her family included taking on responsibility for her parents' lives, which interfered with her normal development. Eve's manipulative coping behavior (refusal to attend school, suicide attempt) served temporarily to reunite her parents as allies and to approximate an underlying fantasy of parental reunion.

The family crisis was formulated in terms of the violation of hierarchial boundaries: Lou and his ex-wife were unable to problem-solve successfully as a parental unit or as separate individuals. This responsibility was (unconsciously) delegated to Eve, who undertook the massive endeavor in her own way—by provoking a crisis.

Art Therapy and Treatment

Cognitive understanding of crisis dynamics

Lou and Eve began their first session by describing the chaotic series of events precipitating their entry to treatment. Initially, Eve identified her refusal to attend school as the basis for this turmoil. Her drawing (Figure 2.8) bypassed this conscious explanation by exposing a core dynamic of her crisis and a significant part of her father's crisis as well. The depiction of her parents' transformation from enemies into allies (before and after the

Figure 2.8.   Eve's wish for parental reunion.

Right now every day is very foggy with constant unknowns + everything seems to be out of control + full of chaos. It's very difficult to find happiness in our situation.

Figure 2.9.   Lou hides in his fog.

crisis precipitant) explicitly expressed her underlying wish for parental re-union. Discussion provoked by this image revealed that Eve's father was unclear about his relationship with her mother—an ambivalence that fueled Eve's reunion fantasy. Thus, Eve's simple drawing provided father and daughter with a cognitive grasp of the crisis and helped to avoid the pitfall of diversion into the chaos surrounding their entry into treatment.

Identification and expression of crisis-related affect

During their second session, Lou and Eve were each asked to choose two magazine collage pictures to describe how they were feeling about their family. Figure 2.9 depicts the car wreck and thick fog that metaphorically expressed Lou's depression, anxiety, and confusion. His written commentary states: ''Right now every day is very foggy with constant unknown and everything seems to be out of control and full of chaos. It's very difficult to find happiness in our situation.'' Drawing upon the revelations of session 1, I assisted Lou to explore how he habitually coped by using the fog (his fear and ambivalence) to perpetuate chaos and avoid underlying issues. Lou was able to clarify that *he* felt out of control and was frightened by his lack of self-definition.

Eve's response to the art intervention showed the image of an exhausted workhorse dragging a heavy piece of machinery. By identifying with this animal, Eve was able to articulate her feelings of sadness and despair. The burden Eve was dragging was eventually recognized by Eve and her father as the heavy weight of her parents' unresolved divorce.

Exploration of previous coping mechanisms and facilitation of adaptive coping through problem-solving

The art intervention discussed in the previous section served the dual purpose of eliciting affect and illuminating the ways in which Lou and Eve coped in their family. Since they had discovered so much about themselves within their metaphors (Lou's fog and Eve's workhorse), the next art intervention utilized these same metaphors to promote adaptive coping.

I asked Lou to choose magazine collage images describing what would appear if the fog lifted (Figure 2.10). His written narrative reads, "Through the fog of the past few weeks things have *started* to clear and a path, still somewhat muddied, can be seen. An objective, or desire, is to have the path cleared and see the light ahead, which to me would symbolize clarity in dealing with (Eve), her mother, and life in general." Through the art process, Lou had risked lifting his protective fog and he began to realize that he had choices. More importantly, Lou recognized that a major choice was to confront his conflict about taking responsibility for his own life.

Eve was asked to use collage images to depict what the workhorse would do if it was released from its harness. Her imagery portrayed jubilance at running wild and free. Influenced by his daughter's artwork, Lou gained painful awareness of how he had unconsciously used Eve to carry his burden. Eve's desire to "run wild" prompted a discussion about freedom within appropriate limits. Lou began to grasp that his role as father demanded that he provide Eve a safe structure in which to thrive.

Figure 2.10.   Lou begins to see more clearly.

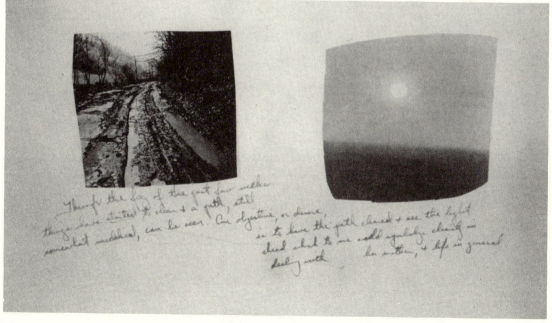

Anticipatory planning

Since Lou and Eve had missed two sessions, we had only one more session in which to further crisis resolution and establish closure. To meet these needs, I employed an art intervention intended to promote problem-solving and encompass some anticipatory planning. Lou and Eve were asked to use drawing or collage to define their choices regarding the family situation. I suggested that they visualize finding options at the ends of different roads.

This intervention facilitated a breakthrough for Lou in problem-solving, as he was able to "possibilize" (Carnes, 1979) his potential for affecting change (Figure 2.11). The centered image of the finger poised to push the button represents Lou's conflict about taking responsibility for his life (caption reads, "Buttons have to be pushed, and the right ones can make a major difference"). Notice how his options stem metaphorically from his ability to push the button.

Figure 2.11.   "Possibilizing" the potential for change.

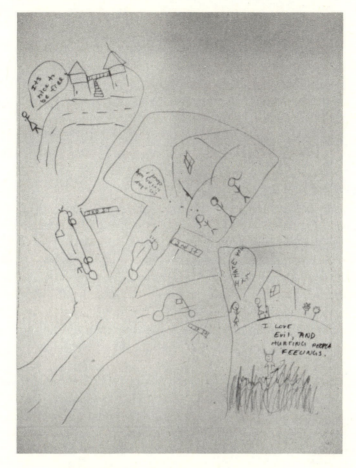

Figure 2.12. Eve explores her choices.

The collage allowed Lou to test out asserting himself, as seen in his strong grasp of the flashlight, accompanied by the caption: "Speaking up and letting Eve's mom hear what I really feel could shed some light . . ." He could also see himself through the metaphor of the plug, which reflects his sense of disconnection, as well as his potential for gaining personal power (caption reads, "This button would put me in charge . . .").

Lastly, through the metaphor of the vicious eel, Lou was finally able to express some of his anger and to visualize himself as aggressively taking control.

Figure 2.12 reveals Eve's drawing in which she delineated three choices: the road on the lower right leads her to an angry confrontation with her stepfather (depicted as the devil); the middle road leads her back to her father; and the road on the upper left leads her to her mother, where the two of them would live without Eve's stepfather. This last road was Eve's most desired option; however, she was enabled to see how this choice was inaccessible, as this road was disconnected from the highway. In the context of this observation Eve was able, for the first time, to clearly discern her wish to protect her mother by driving away her stepfather. Her drawing helped her begin to see that this choice was unattainable and that she was not responsible for her mother's life.

This art intervention assisted Lou and Eve to clarify their options while anticipating how they might respond to upcoming real-life situations.

Summary of gains

Given our limited time, I suggested a review of Lou and Eve's artwork as a means of summarizing gains. This proved to be a powerful reinforcer for Lou, as his sequential collages (Figures 2.9, 2.10, and 2.11) clearly illustrated his metaphorical transformation. Whereas he was initially surrounded by fog, he gained visibility and finally saw himself as directing the light (note the image of the hand firmly holding the flashlight in Figure 2.11). Although it was still conflictual for him to take action, he had attained a cognitive understanding of his personal dilemma and had touched upon his potential to take responsibility for himself as an individual and as a father.

In reviewing her artwork, Eve was struck with how absorbed she was with taking care of her parents. The cumulative effect distressed this 12-year-old, as she felt her loss of participation in normal adolescent development. Lou witnessed this, which strengthened his resolve to relieve Eve of her parentified burden.

CONCLUSION

Art therapy proved to be an invaluable component of family crisis intervention, enhancing the attainment of cognitive understanding, expression of related affect, exploration of previous coping mechanisms, adaptive coping through problem-solving, anticipatory planning, and the summary of gains made during the intervention process.

The visual image worked powerfully to expose underlying crisis dynamics and make them available for verbal exploration. Of particular import was the extraordinary ability of the art modality to spark several crucial areas of inquiry simultaneously. Frequently, a single art expression assisted its creator to gain cognitive understanding, affective release, and a means to explore coping mechanisms. This condensation accelerated the process of crisis resolution and, as such, became an invaluable asset to family crisis intervention—where time is of the essence.

BIBLIOGRAPHY

Aguilera, D. C., & Messick, J. M. (1986). *Crisis Intervention: Theory and Methodology*. St. Louis: C. V. Mosby.

Bonnefil, M. C. (1980). Crisis intervention with children and families. In G.F. Jacobson (Ed.), *Crisis Intervention in the 1980s* (pp. 23–35). San Francisco: Jossey-Bass.

Bonnefil, M. C., & Jacobson, G. F. (1979). Family crisis intervention. *Clinical Social Work Journal, 7*(3), 200–213.

Carnes, J. J. (1979). Toward a cognitive theory of art therapy. *Art Psychotherapy, 6,* 69–75.

Guilliland, B. E., & James, R. K. (1988). *Crisis Intervention Strategies*. Belmont, CA: Wadsworth.

Horowitz, M. J. (1971). Graphic images in psychotherapy. *American Journal of Art Therapy, 10*(3), 153–162.

Jacobson, G. F. (1980a). Crisis theory. In G.F. Jacobson (Ed.), *Crisis Intervention in the 1980s* (pp.1–11). San Francisco: Jossey-Bass.

Jacobson, G. F. (1980b). Editor's notes. In G.F. Jacobson (Ed.), *Crisis Intervention in the 1980s* (pp.#ii–ix). San Francisco: Jossey-Bass.

Landgarten, H. B. (1987). *Family Art Psychotherapy: A Clinical Guide and Casebook*. New York: Brunner/Mazel.

Lindemann, E. (1944). Symptomatology and management of acute grief. *American Journal of Psychiatry, 101*, 141–148.

Morley, W.E. (1980). Crisis intervention with adults. In G.F. Jacobson (Ed), *Crisis Intervention in the 1980s* (pp. 11–23). San Francisco: Jossey-Bass.

Staunton, A. (1982). Art therapy adapted to crisis intervention with adult outpatients. Unpublished thesis. Loyola Marymount University, Art Therapy Department, Los Angeles.

Strickler, M., & Bonnefil, M. (1974). Crisis intervention and social casework: Similarities and differences in problem solving. *Clinical Social Work Journal, 2*(1), 36–44.

Strickler, M., & La Sor, B. (1970). The concept of loss in crisis intervention. *Mental Hygiene, 54*(2), 301–305.

Umana, R. F., Gross, S. J., & McConville, M.T. (1980). *Crisis in the Family*. New York: Gardner Press.

Wadeson, H. (1980). *Art Psychotherapy*. New York: John Wiley.

—3—

Family Art Therapy with Single-Parent Families

Susan Brook

This chapter explores the problems and the art therapy treatment of single-parent families. In particular, I will focus on the use of the art process to impact the generational boundaries within these families, since they are particularly vulnerable to weakened boundaries. These boundaries are the limits between the parent and the children that define the roles and expectations of each generation. The role of a parent is usually seen as an executive function, one of making decisions and rules for the family and maintaining them. Parents also are responsible for providing safe and nurturing homes for the children in which to grow. In single-parent families, the children are suffering from the loss of one parent, as well as, very often, the loss of their former socioeconomic status. The single parent's responsibilities more than double, which may lead to a weakening of the remaining executive system and, in turn, to a breakdown in family organization.

Single-parent families are a relatively recent phenomena. Even the name is new. Until recently, children of divorce were referred to as coming from "broken homes," inspiring images of broken rafters, walls, and chimneys in the mind of a young child. Perhaps this image of a broken home is an accurate metaphor for how society has viewed the divorced family. The parents, who are thought of as usually maintaining a secure and nurturing home for their children, no longer have the means to do that as single parents. The "broken home" refers to the household headed by one parent, which rarely has the same social, economic, familial, and emotional supports it had as an intact family. "Single-parent family" is a term, accepted in the last two decades, that reflects the dramatic rise in divorce rates cutting across all socioeconomic classes.

It is estimated that close to half of this nation's children will spend significant time in single-parent families (Bane, 1976); 90% of these households are headed by women (Wallerstein & Blakeslee, 1989). However, even with this awareness, there is still a strong negative connotation attributed to this newly designated unit. In their book, *Feminist Family Therapy* (1988), Goodrich, Rampage, Ellman, and Halstead write that while men who opt to be the custodial parent are viewed as heroes, admired for their willingness and capacity to do it all, the "single mother is seen as a failure, a suspicious figure who is sometimes pitied but more often criticized for getting herself in this position" (p. 64).

If the modern woman is having difficulty balancing her roles as mother and career woman, the single woman who is also a parent is finding it even more difficult to balance these roles without help from a spouse, often without financial security, and with society offering very little support. When children present to clinics after not doing well in school, it is often found that their mother is so exhausted from her job that it is difficult for the family to have dinner together or for her to have the energy to check their homework. Therapists can be impatient with these single mothers who may seem weak or ineffectual because they lack the emotional resources to be an effective parent (Morawetz & Walker, 1984; Goodrich et al., 1988).

Single-parent families are the most common family configuration presenting at the community mental health clinic where this study was done. Most of these families have little time or money to spend on long-term, insight-oriented therapy. The following case vignette illustrates the plight of the single-parent family. A young mother of two children calls the clinic because she is worried about her six-year-old son. Although he is very bright, he does not listen to her or to his teacher. The mother is immature and not always a consistent role model for the children, but she has responded to her son's behavior in a caring, committed way. Because of their work and school schedules, it is almost impossible to find a convenient time for the family to be seen. The early evening time agreed upon is almost too late for the four-year-old daughter; also, by then, the family is tired. In addition, families like these are usually seen in community mental health clinics by interns who come and go from the agency. Rarely are there funds for long-term therapy. Therefore, the therapist, to help this child (and thousands like him), must recognize all the realities and limitations of therapy with the single-parent family.

The literature on single-parent families presents a bleak picture. Wallerstein and Blakeslee (1989) state that less than half of the families report that the quality of life has improved since the divorce. Follow-up on families for the past 15 years shows the children acting in dysfunctional ways in a blind search for a strong parent to contain their fears, anxieties, and depression. The single parent, usually a woman, is searching for her own identity. She is, in all probability, suffering from numerous losses, including financial status, spousal status, friendships, and familial support by the husband's relatives (Wallerstein & Blakeslee, 1989).

The issues involved in working with single-parent families can be divided into three major catagories: problems the parent faces, problems the children face, and therapy to address these problems. For the newly single parent, no matter how terrible the marriage was, the loss of the bond can be terrifying. The spouses almost always experience strong grief over the loss of the relationship, or at least of their dream of what the relationship could have been. However, they often feel they must be strong and cope, not allowing themselves the luxury of mourning.

This unresolved grief can then develop into the more serious problem of depression in which self-worth is attacked. Children of these families sense their parent's needs and inappropriately try to become the "lost partner," thereby blurring the generational boundaries. A mother in this position may pull the child closer, wishing the youngster to identify with her, or, at the other extreme, will identify one child as like the former spouse and unleash all her fury upon this child, especially a son. While the mother may be in a deep depression, the children become anxious and misbehave, making her take an active position in response to their disobedience (Fulmer, 1983; Weiss, 1976).

Single-parent families often face huge financial problems as well. Most custodial parents are women whose standards of living drop when they divorce. Just getting to work may be a major problem when there is no one to help. Often a mother and her children rely for financial support on the mother's parents, who may even encourage the reliance if they originally opposed the marriage. This help can then lead to a resurgence of the original conflicts between the mother and her parents. It may also weaken the mother's sense of competence at the very time she needs to feel secure in her adult role (Kaplan, 1977).

Lack of organization can be another practical problem for a single parent. The difficulties posed by the often chaotic life of the single-parent family may be compounded by economic hardship, occupational concerns, and disorganized household maintenance.

Women seem to have the most difficulty in setting appropriate routines and formulating rules for the new family unit. In the intact family, it had often been the "man's job" to set the rules. Single fathers with custody also have difficulty because of their new desire to nurture and fill in the "mother's role." Unfortunately, the cycle of the parent unable to say no, the child demanding more, the parent feeling guilty, the child flouting the parent's authority, and the parent feeling fatigued and increasingly helpless usually does not improve with time.

One must also consider the single parent's own needs at this time. The divorced mother is often isolated and feels overburdened by the demands of her new life. If the mother begins to date in order to meet these needs, new problems arise. The most important consideration for the children is their vulnerability to feelings of being rejected or displaced by the mother's new relationships.

The children's needs and issues are as powerful as those of the single parent, but must not be considered separately. Most often, children in those cases misbehave at school and the worried single mother drags the child to therapy, hoping to have a therapist "fix the problem."

The first and most powerful issue for the children is loss: loss of the absent parent, loss of a lifestyle, often loss of home, of school, of neighborhood friends, and, worst of all, loss of the custodial parent's ability to parent. Children, especially young children, are usually the recipient of both parents' love and affection during the troubled marriage. At separation, the custodial parent often becomes depressed and unavailable. As a result, the youngest children suffer loss of both parents, one to divorce and one to depression.

Another psychological factor in single-parent families is that the children and parent become increasingly dependent on each other. Children feel less secure with only one parent and worry that that parent, too, somehow will abandon them.

Studies already cited have shown that children of divorced families are more oppositional, aggressive, lacking in self-control, distractible, and demanding of help both at home and school than children of intact families. Divorced parents have demonstrated feelings of incompetency, anxiety, depression, and abandonment. These feelings improved with time, but the amount of improvement depends on the support systems of the single parent (Hetherington et al., 1978).

While literature about work with single-parent families has been limited, brief structural therapy seems to be the therapy of choice in the studies that are available (Morawetz & Walker, 1984). The literature emphasizes the problems that single mothers face and that result in the chaotic lifestyles of their families (Morrissette, 1987).

Interventions in single-parent families emphasize strengthening the executive system, which now consists solely of the custodial parent. Structural therapy is often stressed in studies that show divorce as unbalancing the family system. Family therapy is appropriate to realign and rebalance the system with a special emphasis on strengthening the executive (remaining) parent (Kaplan, 1977; Rosenthal & Hansen, 1980).

Although many authors discuss structural therapy in their approach to single-parent families, only Glenwick and Mowrey (1986) look specifically at generational boundaries, which pose unique problems in these families. The blurring of boundaries, as Minuchin (1967) described them, is an accurate assessment of many families with the following characteristics: late latency-age child, who typically resides with his or her mother; abdication by the mother of the parental role; parent-child relationship in which the mother functions as a peer/partner.

Therapy involves helping the mother return to her parent role and resolve conflicts, permitting the child to express feelings that are more age-appropriate and modifying the parent-child communication. Minuchin and Fishman (1981) describe how bright, verbal children encourage the mother's abdication of the parental role. The tired mother is often fooled by the "pseudo-maturity" of the child, who demonstrates the ability to listen to a broad range of her personal issues. The message is often, "We're in this together, kid," and an enmeshed mother-child boundary emerges, except that overprotectiveness, normally a feature of enmeshment, is absent for the child.

The problem is that this regression of the mother in service of her own needs often pulls the child to a pseudoadulthood for which he or she is not prepared. The mother may project her attitudes onto her child, telling the therapist, "Johnny doesn't want to see his father," or "Mary doesn't mind being left alone," statements that often represent her own feelings and wishes. The blurring of boundaries creates extra tension and competition in normally competitive mother/daughter relationships when both are dating or both are in school.

Given these problems that plague all single-parent families, Weltner (1982) urges priorities for therapeutic approaches. Mainly, he works to support executive system functions and to establish or strengthen generational boundaries. The first and continuing task is to shore up the beleaguered, fatigued parent. All other interventions hinge on the creation of a strong executive role, and this goal must be persistently pursued. Weltner compares this to the strength of the ego in individual psychotherapy. "Where the ego is sufficiently intact, confrontation and interpretation strengthen the individual and support growth. With a weak ego, however, these same interventions may lead to regression and further fragmentations" (p. 209). Strengthening the single parent is, then, the central focus of all interventions.

Establishing generational boundaries is the second task in Weltner's (1982) work. He lists a variety of ways in which this task can be achieved, including generational labeling of topics and specific seating arrangements in therapy sessions.

Later articles by Lewis (1986) and Morrissette (1987) corroborate the single-parent family's need for a strong executive leader. They found mothers often so afraid of incurring their children's disaffection that they hesitated to exert appropriate controls. Lewis reminds us that the presenting symptom has a protective function for the family. In this way of thinking, the child's problem may help a parent maintain self-control; single parents are particularly vulnerable. Children's problems may specifically serve as protection for single parents. For example, if the child refuses to go to school, the single parent may not have to face up to looking for a job.

Lewis advocates strategic interventions that always support the parental role as the expert and the leader. Morrissette stresses that therapy can create a context in which family members can perceive each other differently, even if for a brief period, and can affect the interpersonal relationships in the future. He writes that a change in one person of the family system can have a rippling effect on the entire family. He agrees with Lewis that criticism of the parent would be counterproductive in avoiding noncompliance. Instead, Morrissette suggests teaching parents, by use of metaphors, to strengthen their executive function in the family hierarchy. However, he cautions the therapist to do so only in a supportive way so that the parent is always the initiator of control.

Clinical art therapy is an effective way to use metaphor to teach parents and children new roles and relationships, thus adding a new dimension to structural family therapy. The art process helps the therapist assess the family patterns. Since the finished products are concrete representations of the family's feelings, communications, and goals, the art therapist can use the art task to intervene in a family system to help realign the family. Landgarten (1987) shows how art tasks help a single-parent family deal with the anger and loss caused by the divorce. She physically intercedes with a depressed mother to have her take charge of an art task, thereby empowering her role.

Riley (1988) describes art therapy's special contribution to family therapy; the art is often the physical receptacle for all the parent's needs and worries. For example, Riley has a mother draw all her worries in a box and leave the picture with the therapist, which allows her to lean on another adult (the therapist) for support instead of turning to a child.

The problems of a single-parent family are not going to be easily solved by any type of therapy, but this population presents one of the most significant and pressing needs of society. The lack of positive public opinions concerning single-parent families only makes the task more difficult. Art therapy can serve as a shortcut to, and yet deeply touch, the needs of a single mother and her children.

The work of the family art therapist is to assess the family members' needs and weaknesses and help them grow to meet the new challenges that being in a single-parent family creates. The remainder of this chapter will discuss how art therapy interventions were used to meet those challenges for two single-parent families seen weekly for three to nine months.

CASE STUDIES

The A Family

The A family called the clinic on their priest's advice. The mother, Molly, was worried about her 11-year-old daughter, Heather, who was acting withdrawn, fearful, and depressed. There were two other children in the family, Kelly, aged seven, and Brendan, aged four. Molly expressed fears that her older daughter was like the father, whom Mrs. A had left six months earlier after years of verbal and physical abuse. She and the children moved to a shelter for battered women and then to public housing.

There was a restraining order against the father and the family had no contact with him or their former neighborhood, schools, or friends. Heather had always been quiet and shy, but since the separation, these characteristics had increased to the point that she was afraid of all men. The family had never been in therapy and was reluctant to try it, but Molly took her priest's advice and sought help for Heather.

Aside from their church, the family had few sources of support. The family members had no contact with the father or with his family. Mrs. A's own parents were dead, and only her grandmother and a sister remained in the family's lives. Mrs. A had no close women friends and no desire to get close to a man. She was a full-time nursing student, and her college and professors were very important to her. Her main source of income was from government aid to dependent children.

Even with all the trauma and lack of resources, the family was still highly functioning. The children were doing well in school and, except for Heather, beginning to make new friends. Mrs. A was also doing well in school, although she felt overwhelmed at times by the school work and the responsibilities of single parenthood. This family was very close and its members spent most of their free time together.

Molly and her three children arrived at the clinic, all very shy, polite, and nervous. Heather was very quiet, but would smile in a sweet, embarrassed way when I spoke to her. Kelly did not speak, but looked at everything in the room and watched everyone's reactions. Brendan clung closely to his mother.

I knew that the family had suffered many losses through the separation and moves, so I assured the children, particularly Heather, that therapy would not separate them, that they would not be taken away from their mother or from each other. Responding to their obvious relief, which indicated their lack of security, I asked Heather to draw a very safe place. She

Figure 3.1. ''A safe place.''

drew a ''beautiful house,'' which became the metaphor for the family's security (Figure 3.1).

Within the first session, it was clear that Heather was very bright and sensitive and that her depression was her response to the family's trauma. I believed she was the ''family receptacle'' for all the fear and depression from their losses.

During the next few sessions, other family dynamics were discussed. Molly set limits and maintained them. She had high expectations for the children's behavior, manners, and help with the house. She particularly depended on Heather, who often cared for the younger children while Molly was at class. However, Molly's executive ability was less effective in the emotional area. She was unaware of her own feelings. It was painful for her to remember anything about her husband and she actively denied any emotional response to the separation. It was in that arena that her daughter was responding.

My original hypothesis of their dynamics was:

The mother kept the father alive by associating his behavior with the elder daughter. Heather's withdrawn, depressed behavior reflected Molly's and the other children's depression and fears.

My original therapeutic goals were to:
1. Separate Heather from her father in the mother's eyes.

2. Support and strengthen the mother as a single parent, since the feelings of self-worth of battered women are diminished.
3. Assess the structure of this newly formed single-parent family and firm the generational boundaries to support the executive of the parent.

Interventions

My first goal was to create a safe place in the therapeutic relationship. This meant building a trusting relationship with the clinic and with me. Verbally, I assured them that therapy would not separate them, that this clinic helped keep families together, and that the "safe place" art task allowed them to create a concrete object that would be hung on the wall of the art therapy room to be seen every time they entered. They would see Heather's beautiful, grounded home. The art itself could become a consistent object in their life.

The younger children copied Heather's idea of a house, and from this I developed the theme of a house to become the metaphor for their security. To punctuate the reality of the separation and changes, I asked the family to draw what their home was like before their moves and what it was like now. They each were to do this drawing on two sides of a paper. Keeping in mind the goal to strengthen the mother/parental role as separate and more powerful than the children, I gave the mother a special role in the art tasks. To support the mother as the leader, I asked her to be in charge of taking the pictures in each category and arranging them in two collages. This move was a symbol of mother's role as the executive decision-maker.

Figure 3.2. "A strong home."

The most concrete of the "safe houses" was the three dimensional construction that the children created out of construction paper while mom was away with the co-therapist discussing the extent of the abuse. I asked the children to make a "beautiful house" together out of construction paper, to which they added their personal touches in their own bedroom windows. The house was very flimsy until Molly joined the children, and I asked her to make it stronger. While she designed and created supports to increase the sturdiness of the house, I emphasized mother's special role in making the structure "very strong so nothing could happen to it." During that time, the children were given the job of creating a garden and places to play outside. Here the mother's role was the protector while the children were busy with children's work—play (Figure 3.2).

With each of these therapeutic moves of placing the mother in charge of organization and safety, Molly worked with pride and satisfaction as her children watched her complete the task for the family. Each time, the children became quiet while mother took over the executive role. Heather, the identified patient, seemed to relax, smile, and become like the other kids. Kelly stopped being the family reporter and followed her mother's directions. Brendan sat still and worked on his art contribution.

Another important area which affected this family's organization was Molly's low sense of self-worth. Although she was going to school and raising three children on her own, she had been a battered woman. Her decision to leave her husband had been a difficult and long one. She had little support. She needed validation as a decision-maker. With the children, she was almost too strict, as if her firm control could mask her deep fear and insecurity.

Early in the therapy, I attended to Molly's insecurity by an art directive that enhanced her accomplishments and her value to the family. She had come in for one session overwhelmed and tired from studying for midterms. I drew a large outline of a woman and asked the family to "cut out and paste on the paper all the pictures from the collage box that show everything Mom is and what she does." The entire family attacked this project with glee. As the children picked photos, they each made comments like, "Mommy, you do that, Mommy wears beautiful clothes, Mommy exercises, Mommy makes us food," and "Oh, Mommy, you can go out on a date." Mommy beamed or blushed with every comment.

The collage was full and very large. Molly departed with a new image of herself. In place of the image of a harried, exhausted, depressed woman, the family reframed her role as one of strength, beauty, warmth, and accomplishment. Once again, all the family members had an important, active role, but Mother's was different and separate from the younger generation; she was the object of the work. While this art intervention separated the

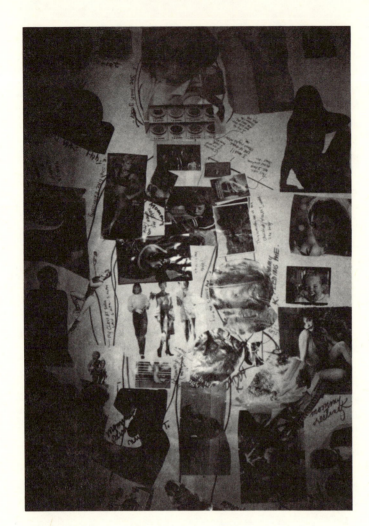

Figure 3.3.
"All about Mom."

Figure 3.4. "Our family Thanksgiving."

generations, it also united the family by the mother seeing the children's appreciation of her and the children seeing the powerful parent they had (Figure 3.3).

After the first six weeks of therapy, Heather was doing much better. She would come bouncing into therapy describing her new friends and the parties she was attending; we all wondered where the depressed, frightened girl had gone. Jokingly, I told her to go to her room and be depressed, so we could all continue therapy. Everyone's response to this was to laugh, particularly Heather.

It was close to Thanksgiving and I used this opportunity to continue to help strengthen the mother in this newly reconstituted family. It would be the first major holiday without the father. I told them how I admired them for their ability to do so well with all the changes, but I stressed that holidays were a difficult time for any family with sad memories. It was normal, I emphasized, to feel sad or miss the people we have lost, and I wondered out loud if they were thinking about their father. They immediately told me that they were thinking that this holiday would be better without him because he had not liked all the fuss and preparations for the holidays.

I used their own history to develop the art task. I asked them to create anything out of plasticene that made them think of Thanksgiving. The children went immediately to work, using all their knowledge from school about the special foods and symbols. I asked Molly to make the tablecloth for all these symbols and told her that she could decorate and shape it any way she wanted. Once again, I gave her a special role to give shape and form to her family activity (Figure 3.4).

It is important to state that Molly's three children were active and excited about doing all of the art projects. They immediately began work and enthusiastically reached for supplies. There was some competition in all the tasks about who did what and who got to use what supplies, but not between the mother and children when the mother was given a special role in each task. That special job always separated the children from Mother and allowed both the children and the mother to see the parent as the leader in a way that was understandable to children of any age.

In order to evaluate the present family dynamics after five months of therapy, I directed the family to do a group art task. I asked them to make a group sculpture out of construction paper without designating a special role for the mother. The mother's work was the most dominating and decorative, but it was not connected to the others. She created her lovely trees by herself and didn't offer to work with the children. Heather also worked independently. Only Kelly tried to organize the other children. Brendon came to me for help (Figure 3.5).

Figure 3.5. "The family garden."

In evaluating this family's progress through therapy, I was struck by certain characteristics. The original presenting problem not only had ceased to be a problem, but five months later Molly came into therapy telling me that she realized that when she first called for help, she was worried about her daughter, Heather. Then she wondered if "really, it was just everything I was going through" and maybe there wasn't anything wrong with her daughter. Art therapy is not verbal and patients interpret only what they are ready to see. Because she came to that understanding by herself, she was able to integrate this comprehension as part of her own growth.

Since therapy first sought to give support and security to the identified patient, Heather, Molly was free to look at her own losses and needs. At the same time, while therapy always paid attention to supporting the single parent, it freed the children to worry less about adult problems and concentrate on their work in school and on friends. In structural terms, the mother ceased to be enmeshed. Therapy separated the generations by clarifying the generational roles, but unified the newly formed single-parent family, giving each member the chance to be age-appropriate.

At that point in therapy, the A family was more stable and high functioning. Molly felt more sure of herself and the children were less fearful and depressed. Molly's style was slightly disengaged, which was probably due to her struggles to become strong and independent. That was something to be aware of as the children grew into adolescence and began to need deeper communication.

The B Family

The B family began family therapy with me after they had been seen at the crisis clinic for six sessions by another art therapist. That work began after Mrs. B, Sarah, was physically attacked by her husband. The event was precipitated by Sarah's telling her husband that she was pregnant and that she refused to get an abortion. Eight-year-old Hillary and her four-year-old brother, Tommy, had called 911 for help to save their mother from their father. Mr. B was arrested and moved out of the house, and divorce proceedings were begun.

When Hillary heard her mother planning a visit for the children with their father, she became hysterical. At that point, they came to the crisis center of our clinic. The mother reported that the father had often abused her, was an alcoholic, and had many firearms. He had also hurt Hillary in the past by kicking her and pulling her hair. He insisted that the whole family watch violent movies together. The therapist at the time filed an abuse report. The family had been to the crisis center many times over the past three years for abuse, and had formed a trusting relationship with the clinic.

The focus of the six sessions of crisis work was to support and strengthen the battered mother. She admitted that she was "like one of the children," and that she often relied on Hillary and Tommy to take care of her and protect her from her husband. The original hypothesis of the crisis work was that Hillary's psuedo-maturity was due to her mother's immaturity. The parental role was too difficult for Hillary and causing much distress and dysfunction.

At the time they entered family therapy with me, both children were still showing signs of fearfulness and distrust. Hillary's affect seemed almost flat and she was anxious and fearful. Tommy was also suffering from the trauma he had witnessed. He, too, did not want to see his father, was afraid the father would kidnap them, and was wakeful at night with nightmares, a need to urinate often, and worries that something would happen to his mother. On three different occasions when they had visited their father, something frightening had happened, including the father stealing important papers from the mother at gunpoint.

While the mother readily spoke of the children's need to be children and not her protectors, she was not yet able to provide them with the security necessary for them to be able to let down their vigilance. Sarah spoke openly in front of the children, even about the details of the abuse. Until the separation, the father had made all the decisions and had set all the limits and rules, which he maintained by fear and brutality. He insisted that all three of them go to bed at eight p.m. Also, they were not allowed to have friends in their home or to visit the homes of their friends.

A support system for this family was almost nonexistent. Sarah's family, immigrants from Mexico, lived in New Mexico and had little money. Her husband's family felt she was beneath them because of her heritage. She was close to one older couple, who lent her money for a lawyer and food.

Even with the terrible stress and trauma that the young children had witnessed, they were functioning well in school. Hillary was beginning to make friends, and was even thinking of planning a slumber party. She used to lie to her friends about why they could not visit, as she was afraid of her father's drunken rages. Tommy was happy at his nursery school. However, both children seemed shy and unfriendly at the beginning of the first session. Sarah, too, was a highly functioning woman. Although she was single with two children and pregnant, she was continuing to attend college full time.

The major dysfunction for this family centered around relating to the father. Both the children and the mother were very afraid of him. This fear created strong bonds between the mother and the children, but also blurred the generational boundaries. Since the mother had no support system, she relied on the children as her allies. In turn, the children felt a need to protect her, which precluded their normal development.

My original hypothesis was:

The children's pseudomaturity was a defense against their great insecurity about their mother's inability to protect them and herself. The mother responded to their strength by being more passive and immature. Hillary's crying about the visits to the father was her way of activating her mother to take care of her. Hillary and Tommy's pseudomature behavior was a mask for their deep fear of their father. Their hysteria activated their mother to change her passive, frightened stance and seek therapy.

My original goals of therapy were to:
1. Provide the mother with enough support to protect her children.
2. Help the mother with her feelings of self-worth so as to validate her decision to leave an abusive husband.
3. Provide the family members with a safe place in the therapy so that they could explore their feelings about their past trauma.

Interventions

The first session with Sarah's family produced many clues to their dynamics. The art directive was to "Divide your paper in half. On one side pick out some pictures that show how you feel when you say 'Goodbye'; on the other, paste some pictures that show how you feel when you say 'Hello.' "

On one level, this was to acknowledge their change from the other art therapist to me. On another, they were dealing with a greater loss, their father.

Sarah's drawing showed an island for her goodbye picture, writing about how alone and isolated she felt when she said "Goodbye," but that "Hellos" were like new flowers. Hillary's photos were humorous, using story characters saying "Goodbye" or "Hello." Tommy chose cartoon characters that were amazingly appropriate for the concepts. Sarah picked beautiful images devoid of humans or animals. I knew she was a battered woman who felt no trust in any person. (Figure 3.6)

Sarah's family was in the middle of continuing stress in a custody and visitation battle at the time of intake and I knew safety was foremost on their minds. At an early session, I asked each of them to draw a safe place. Sarah drew the three of them in a cloud with a ladder that one could pull into the cloud. Hillary's safe place was the three of them on a hill with nothing around. Interestingly, Tommy's was the most protective. He drew a shield and then a cheetah, which said, "This is a mommy cheetah. Her job is to keep the house safe." (Sarah had many freckles.)

While the family was discussing their drawings, little Tommy started scribbling on Hillary's drawing. Hillary told him to stop, almost too nicely. I encouraged her to speak to him more strongly, to relax her rigid control, and to take care of her own needs. At that point, he looked up and said, "I'm

Figure 3.6. "New beginnings."

GOODBYE

||HELLO!||

LONELY
ISOLATED
MIXED FEELINGS

NEW START
SPRING
BLOSSOM
SEEDS TO NEW RELATIONSHIP

A CLOUD WITH A PRIVATE STEPS TO
RETRIEVE FROM EVERYTHING,

Where up on a h Thingking-
Good Thouths.

This is a mommy Cretan.
Her job is to keep the nouse
safe.

Figure 3.7.
"Protected places."

drawing a shield around us." Tommy seemed to be initiating a common art therapy process in which the client is encouraged to change the reality on the paper. I asked Sarah how she felt about her children's drawings and she told them that it was not their job to keep them safe, but hers (Figure 3.7).

It is important to note that much of the previous six sessions of crisis work in art therapy had been focused on strengthening the mother in order for her to go forward with divorce proceedings and protect her children. She was a very bright and insightful woman who was able to use the imagery as strong messages. With each week of therapy, she became less and less defended as she strove to understand the dynamics of a battered woman.

However, after a particularly upsetting court hearing on visitation, I decided to allow the family to express their anger and frustration in a family mural about the court. It was clear that the children were once again more willing than the mother to stand up and fight. She was angry and drew a symbol for the husband as a big lizard. The children, however, chose more protective means. Hillary maturely wrote words that she wished she could have said to the judge, while Tommy drew a tank. He said he would drive the tank into the courtroom to "pick up my Mom and my Mom's lawyer and the judge and Hillary." It was not surprising that, under stress, this family, who had experienced years of abuse, would revert to their old emotional patterns. I knew it would take continuing processing and reinterpretation of their dynamics to help them experience their new roles (Figure 3.8).

In choosing an image to create a three-dimensional place of safety for this family, I recalled Sarah's first picture of an island, which was how she felt when she said "Goodbye." I chose the island symbol because it came from the mother, whom I was trying to empower. During the court hearings on visitations and custody, the family desperately wanted to feel safe and isolated from the world. Specifically, I asked the mother to create the island and the main house, while the children could make the plants and play structures. That move put the mother in charge of "shaping" their home, their base, their security.

Sarah created a large, simple island, which I thought would be suitable for a main house, while the children created several other structures, perhaps signifying special places for them. However, Sarah built such a large house that it covered most of the island. I silently wondered if there was any space left for the children. At that time, Sarah was also blossoming with positive

Figure 3.8. "The courtroom."

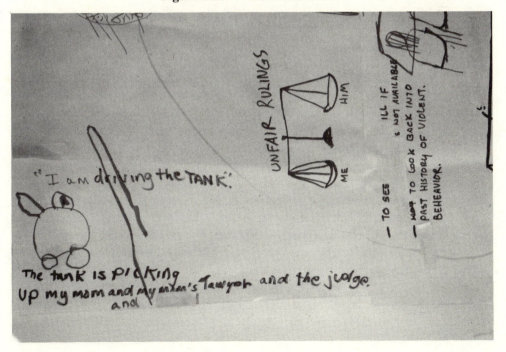

Figure 3.9. "Our own safe island."

energy and stories that took up most of the time in session. I had to make time (room) for the children. I commented about how large the house was, that it had plenty of room for the children to be safe and comfortable. Hillary made a boat for her special place and said she would use it to play, but that she wanted to "stay with my Mom." Tommy made the tree with lots of fruit so that everyone would have enough to eat.

The next week Sarah brought in heavy cardboard to make the house sturdy and she and the children each made themselves out of plasticene. Then, Hillary created another figure who was allowed to visit, a representation of this therapist. One day, after a particularly frightening visit from the father, Tommy created a lion, placed it in front of the door to the house, and put all three family figures inside the house (Figure 3.9).

After one month, this family used art therapy as their safe place to express their fears and anger. The children were still guarded and unwilling to trust that they would be safe. They had more court hearings to attend and their future was uncertain. Their biggest fear was that they would be taken from their mother. However, Sarah was beginning to assume an adult role. She spoke like a fighter when it came to the legal battle. She felt very proud of her independence. She was happy to be doing normal things with the children that they were not allowed to do before, like having slumber parties, joining baseball teams, and visiting friends.

SUMMARY

The therapeutic interventions of creating a safe environment, empowering the single parent, firming the generational boundaries, and encouraging the expression of feelings are valuable in addressing issues with all single-parent families. Although many such families have not left an abusive spouse, whatever changes have occurred have caused a sense of loss and insecurity. The single parent always needs support because she is alone. The boundaries are almost always weak and the roles confused. Therapy can provide safe expression of feelings for the strained family system; art dramatically enhances that process.

The two families contacted the clinic because of a presenting problem with one of the children. Eleven-year-old Heather A was anxious, fearful, and depressed after her mother left Heather's abusive father. Eight-year old Hillary B was anxious and afraid of visiting her father. Both mothers acted out of concern to get therapy for their children. They believed the children were the ones with the emotional problems. Although they felt guilty and worried that their marital situations had caused the dysfunctions, neither realized how connected their own role in the family was to the symptom.

The identified patients were dysfunctional in some way. Both were depressed, manifesting as anger and fear. The other children in each family appeared normal, but they also shared some of the depression, although to a lesser degree. It is important to note that neither child had severe pathology or serious diagnoses that would have required more in-depth work. These children were not suffering from severe emotional illness; their families were suffering from the stress of divorce. The support that marriage provides was abruptly cut off from the families. The stress on the remaining parent to provide financially, emotionally, and physically for her children was too great and the children were the receptors of this stress. These two children, both the eldest in their families, both very bright and verbal, were very sensitive to their mother's needs. They both woried about her security and happiness.

Heather and Hillary were the ''symptom bearers'' for their families. The mother's executive ability in each family was weakened by the stress of changing roles and by years of abuse or criticism. Now that the father was out of the house, there was a vacuum in the power role. The mothers had been the nurturers and were unfamiliar with being the leaders or disciplinarians. They had not been able to be the protectors, even of themselves. Unconsciously, these two children sensed that vacuum, that need, and filled it in inappropriate ways, acting out of fear and depression. However, their dysfunctions served a crucial purpose in their families. Their symptoms catalyzed their mothers to assume the executive position by initiating a call for help.

In both cases, the impact of the art therapy was clear. The specific art tasks were designed as structural moves to empower the parent. The safe places—the house and the island—were protected or strengthened by the mother. The art work served as a concrete enactment for new roles in the family. Rather than tell these women to be strong executives, I asked them to play key roles in the art tasks. They worked in metaphor, taking over the jobs they were assigned in the art.

To firm the generational boundaries, the adults were always asked to organize the art project. Mrs. A was encouraged to organize the two-houses collage, the Thanksgiving plate, and the dreamlike paper sculpture. Mrs. B was asked to construct the island and the house.

Not only could the mothers view their new leadership role in the art, but so could the children. Often the children wanted to create the items the mothers were asked to make, but I encouraged the mothers to stop their children by telling them, "Only Moms can make the. . . ." For the most part, however, the children, especially the identified patients, eagerly watched their mothers in the leadership roles first and then got to work on their own jobs.

Both families showed improvement and both of the children were doing better. Heather A, while still a quiet and polite child, was no longer depressed and withdrawn. Mrs. A was clearly defined in her mother role at intake and even more so after therapy. Family B used art therapy to achieve its goals. The children's anxiety decreased as the mother became more powerful. While designing the large home on the island, she freely spoke of how happy she was to be "the master of my fate." Her comment about the benefits of art therapy was: "No matter how frazzled I am when I come to art therapy, there is something about the creative process that settles me down and makes me realize that my problems are not insurmountable. It's sort of like going to church."

This chapter hypothesizes that empowerment of the adult should alleviate the children's need to act out in symptomatic ways. In both cases, the presenting symptoms diminished. Family art therapy was used in this clinical work to make powerful changes for the family. The visual images of the mother's strength separated and validated her role as the executive, the leader, the protector, the provider. The support given by the therapist and the art together allowed her to take the leadership role more easily without feeling so alone.

The addition of family art therapy to structural theory adds richness, depth, and, hopefully, speed. Certainly, many of the art productions reflect the unconcious desires and fears of all the family members. In structural family art therapy, this understanding of the visual imagery can be transferred to the understanding of the roles and dynamics within the family. For example, it was not necessary to interpret Mrs. B's oversized house in analytical terms. What was important was its expression of strength and how the children could play safely in it and not worry about any typhoons knocking it down.

No matter how few resources these families possessed, emotionally or financially, the significance of the art tasks was not lost on them. Through a very pleasurable activity, the entire family was able to perceive themselves more securely with a clear and strong leader, the single parent. Rather than intellectually understanding what the appropriate roles in a family are, these families were given a chance to enact these roles with no expectation or judgment. Art heals on a primary, nonverbal level; it can reach deeper than the intellect. These families were in great need of healing from the traumas they had suffered. The art tasks were able to soothe and to teach without words.

BIBLIOGRAPHY

Ackerman, N. (1978). *The Psychodynamics of Family Life.*

Bane, M. (1976); Marital disruption in the lives of children. *Journal of Social Issues, 32*(1).

Bateson, G., (1979). *Mind and Nature.* New York: E. P. Dutton.

Bowen, M. (1978). *Family Therapy in Clinical Practice.* New York: Jason Aronson.

Fulmer, R. (1983). A structural approach to unresolved mourning in single-parent family systems. *Journal of Marital and Family Therapy, 9*(3), 259–269.

Glenwick, D., & Mowrey, J. (1986). When parent becomes peer: Loss of intergenerational boundaries in single-parent families. *Family Relations, 35,* 57–62.

Goldenberg, H., & Goldenberg I., (1990). *Counseling Today's Families.* Belmont, CA: Brooks/Cole.

Goodrich, T. J., Rampage, C., Ellman, B., & Halstead, K., (1988). *Feminist Family Therapy: A Casebook.* New York: W.W. Norton.

Greene, K. L. (1977). A pilot study: Differential cultural effects upon the single-parent child demonstrated in artwork. *Art Psychotherapy, 4,* 149–158.

Hayley, J. (1987). *Problem-Solving Therapy.* San Francisco: Jossey-Bass.

Hayley, J., & Hoffman, L. (1967). *Techniques of Family Therapy.* New York: Basic Books.

Hetherington, E. M., Cox, M., & Cox, R. (1978). The aftermath of divorce. In J. H. Stevens, Jr. & M. Matthews, (Eds.), *Mother-Child, Father-Child Relations.* Washington, DC: National Association for the Education of Young Children.

Junge, M. (1985). ''The book about Daddy dying'': A preventive art therapy technique to help families deal with the death of a family member. *Art Therapy, 3,* 4–10.

Kaplan, S. (1977). Structural family therapy. *Family Process, 16,* 75–83.

Kramer, E. (1971). *Art as Therapy with Children.* New York: Schocken Books.

Kwiatkowska, H. Y. (1967a). Family art therapy. *Family Process, 6*(1), 37–55.

Kwiatkowska, H. Y. (1967b). The use of families' art productions for psychiatric evaluation. *Bulletin of Art Therapy, 6,* 52–69.

Kwiatkowska, H. Y. (1975). Family art therapy: Experiments with a new technique. In E. Ulman (Ed.), *Art Therapy in Theory and Practice*. New York: Schocken Books.

Landgarten, H. (1981). *Clinical Art Therapy: A Comprehensive Guide*. New York: Brunner/Mazel.

Landgarten, H. (1987). *Family Art Therapy: A Clinical Guide and Casebook*. New York: Brunner/Mazel.

Levick, M. (1973). *Family Art Therapy in the Community*. 257–261.

Lewis, W. (1986). Strategic interventions with children of single-parent families. *The School Counselor, 33*(5), 375–378.

Madanes, C. (1981). *Strategic Family Therapy*. San Francisco: Jossey-Bass.

Minuchin, S. (1967). *Families of the Slums*. New York: Basic Books.

Minuchin, S., & Fishman, H. (1981). *Family Therapy Techniques*. Cambridge, MA: Harvard University Press.

Moen, H. (1981). *Art Psychotherapy with the Child of Divorce*. Unpublished manuscript, Loyola Marymount University, Los Angeles.

Morawetz, A., & Walker, G. (1984). *Brief Therapy with Single-Parent Families*. New York: Brunner/Mazel.

Morrissette, P. (1987). Altering problematic family hierarchy: A strategy for therapy with single-parent families. *Family Therapy, 14*(1), 53–59.

Naumberg, M. (1966). *Dynamically Oriented Art Therapy: Its Principles and Practices*. New York: Grune & Stratton.

Reilly, J. (1985). *Structural Family Art Therapy: A Clinical Paper*. Unpublished manuscript, Loyola Marymount University, Los Angeles.

Riley, S. (1985). Draw me a Paradox? Family art psychotherapy utilizing a systemic approach to change. *Art Therapy, 9*, 116–123.

Riley, S. (1988). Adolescence and family art therapy: Treating the "adolescent family" with family art therapy. *Art Therapy, 7*, 43–51.

Rosenthal, D., & Hansen, J. (1980). Working with single-parent families. *Family Therapy 7*(2), 73–82.

Sherr, C., & Hicks, H. (1973). Family drawing as a diagnostic and therapeutic technique. *Family Process, 14*, 439–460.

Smead, J. (1981). *Art Therapy as a Support System for Single Mothers: A Proposal*. Unpublished manuscript, Loyola Marymount University, Los Angeles.

Wallerstein, J. S., & Blakeslee, S. (1989). *Second Chances: Men, Women, & Children, a Decade After Divorce*. New York: Ticknor & Fields.

Wallerstein, J. S., & Kelly, J. B. (1977). *Surviving the Breakup: How Children and Parents Cope with Divorce*. New York: Doubleday.

Weiss, R. (1976). The emotional impact of marital separation. *Journal of Social Issues, 32*(1), 135–145.

Weltner, J. (1982). A structural approach to the single-parent family. *Family Process, 21*, 203–210.

Wolfe, G. (1982). *Art Therapy with Only-Child Early Adolescent Boys of Divorce*. Unpublished manuscript, Loyola Marymount University, Los Angeles.

—4—

Art Therapy with Alcoholic Families

Gayle M. Callaghan

Alcoholism has been defined as a person's experiencing significant impairment that is directly associated with the consumption of alcohol. The impairment may involve psychological, physical, or social dysfunction. Alcoholism is characterized by a loss of control over one's drinking that results in problems in job, school, financial affairs, relationships with family and friends, and/or physical health. The alcoholic continues to drink despite the fact that he or she recognizes the existence of a problem that is caused or exacerbated by the drinking or is aware of the danger of alcohol use in situations that may be physically hazardous (such as when driving or when operating equipment).

Deutsche (1982) points out that two out of every three Americans consume alcohol. Black (1981), moreover, notes that of this majority, one out of every six families may be affected by a member's alcoholism. According to Leiken (1986), based on a population of 9 to 13 million alcoholics in the United States, alcoholism touches the lives of some 34 to 52 million family members; it is related to 40 percent of the traffic fatalities, one-half of the arrests, and a large percentage of hospitalizations. Alcoholism is, therefore, not solely a problem a problem of the individual or the family, but one of society as a whole. This involvement of families is termed ''co-dependency,'' and it carries implicit rules about how family members both cope with and work to conceal the alcoholism.

The concern over the effects of parental alcoholism is not new. Warner and Rosett's (1975) review of the history of parental drinking shows that even the ancient Greek philosophers discussed the problem, but it was not until the early 1900s that the neglect of children was first examined as a side effect of parental alcoholism.

Attention to the problem of alcoholism had waxed and waned until about

50 years ago when two alcoholics recognized the value of mutual support in controlling their "disease" and established Alcoholics Anonymous (AA) and its 12-Step programs for recovery. Expanding on this, Alanon, Alateen, and other mutual-support groups were started in the 1950s, followed by the Adult Children of Alcoholics (ACOA or ACA) in the 1970s. With the success of AA, the 12-Step format has expanded to include many other addictions, such as drugs, overeating, sex, and even "workaholism." As word spread about the healing that takes place in the testimonial-style setting of these support groups, victims of the addictions began to see the possibility of help through their peers. Now, chapters of AA and related programs can be found throughout the country and internationally as well.

In the early 1970s, as the problem went "public," the scientific community and society in general saw the need to explore the physiological, genetic, and psychological effects of alcoholism in families. The attitude changed from focusing on alcoholism as a problem of the individual to alcoholism as a disease of the family. Treatment goals currently relate to alleviating the family's sense of suffering in isolation as its members helplessly perpetuate inappropriate roles and pathological communication patterns.

This chapter shows how art therapy can be an effective modality for clearly defining the pathological family interactions and poor communication patterns that foster unhealthy and problematic behavior in its members. Once revealed, this information offers a foundation for therapeutic intervention, which can allow a "shift" in the family dynamics toward healthier, healing patterns.

THE ALCOHOLIC FAMILY

Just as there are different levels in the severity of one's alcoholism, there are also levels of the severity of disruption it causes in the home environment. While some alcoholic families may be marked by only a few of the characteristics described below, others will include many or all. But whatever the level of alcoholism in the family, the members are usually so rigidly bound by their patterns of interaction that some outside intervention is required for them to make changes toward healing. The intervention may come in the form of a psychotherapist, a self-help group (such as AA), or, ideally, a combination of the two.

Because of the centricity of alcoholism within family interaction, the presence of an alcoholic creates an alcoholic family. Stark (1987) describes the atmosphere of an alcoholic home as being permeated with anxiety, tension, confusion, denial, low self-confidence, fear, isolation, and a pact of silence. These traits stem from the family's attempt to cope with the toxic environment created by the alcoholic's behavior. Black (1981) adds that, although a clear indicator of a smoothly working family is consistency, living in an alcoholic family means enduring inconsistency and unpredictability. Deutsche (1982) refers to the alcoholic's inconsistent behavior as a "Dr. Jekyll and Mr. Hyde" effect. Children in these families must attempt to make sense of a situation in which behavior that is acceptable one day may be punishable the next.

Table 4.1 lists characteristics common to alcoholic family members. In the process of researching this topic, it became clear that the most common defense mechanism of alcoholics and their families is denial.

Black (1981) tells us that the denial in alcoholic households takes the form of three basic rules: "Don't talk. Don't trust. Don't feel." These rules are manifested in the following ways.

For family members to talk to outsiders about the alcoholism would shame the family by calling attention to the fact that it has a "problem." The facade of normality is maintained at the high price of members not being allowed to seek help with coping. Distortion and selective "filtering" of information are characteristic communication patterns within the alcoholic family.

In order to perpetuate their facade, members may need to change or reverse their roles. A co-dependent spouse may take responsibility for the alcoholic by making excuses to others for the alcoholic partner's continued absences or poor performance. A parentified child may learn to take care of himself or herself, and the alcoholic parent as well, by cooking, cleaning, paying bills, and keeping the house running. The co-dependent spouse is too focused on coping with the alcoholic to acknowledge the child's humiliation at the parent's showing up at a ballgame drunk, the child's disappointment over forgotten promises, or the child's fear of riding in a car with an inebriated parent. Neither parent can be depended on for support or safety.

Co-dependents are implicitly instructed to ignore the problem in the hope that it will go away. Family members are also not allowed to speak to one another about their thoughts and feelings. Instead, the stronger message is, "Don't rock the boat." If, for example, a child experiences discomfort because his or her drunken father has passed out with his head in his dinner plate, by ignoring the incident, the mother is implying, "What drunk? What problem?" Children learn that their sense that a situation is "not OK" is negated by the family's refusal to acknowledge or correct the problem.

Following a long period of regular adherence to the "Don't talk" rule, children may begin to doubt their own judgment, or possibly even their sanity. This doubt often spills over into other areas, as in finding it difficult to make decisions or feeling a sense of helplessness, traits that can continue into adulthood.

TABLE 4.1
Characteristics of Members in Alcoholic Families

Affect	*Thought*
Anxiety, tension	Confusion, helplessness
Vague fears, phobias	No sense of control
Fear of isolation	Guilt
Disappointment, shame	Worry, being overly serious
Sadness, depression	Harsh self-judgment
Rage, tantrums	Low self-esteem
Presence of mood disorders	Lack of confidence

Presence of Denial	*Individual Performance*
Blaming, instilling guilt	Difficulty expressing feelings
Information filtering	Difficulty with intimacy
Selective memory	Difficulty completing tasks
"Don't talk; don't trust; don't feel"†	Rigid inflexibility
Not allowed to disagree	Overly controlling
Lying when it is as easy to tell the truth	Impulsive behavior
Undeserved loyalty given	Overly responsible or irresponsible
Making excuses for alcoholic's poor	behavior
functioning	Feeling different, out of place
	Stance of helplessness

Roles of Dependents	*Performance in Children* *(additional traits)*
Responsible one*/family hero†	Hyperactivity
Adjusters*/lost child†	Stuttering/stammering
Placater*/mascot†	Trouble in school
Acting-out child*/scapegoat†	Fighting with peers and neighbors
Role reversal (parentified child)	Antisocial behavior
Role confusion	Next-generation substance abuse
Antisocial role modeling	

Family Interaction and Structure	
Inconsistency	Stance of helplessness
Unpredictability	Nagging, coercion, blaming
Lack of dependable support	Centricity of alcoholism
Boundary ambiguity	Double, mixed, or unclear communication
Skewed alliances	patterns
Homeostasis maintained by the identified	Broken and forgotten promises
patient's symptom (deflecting attention	Sibling conflict
from the alcoholism)	Lack of communication between siblings
Infantilized child to maintain enmeshment	Verbal abuse
with co- dependent or "enabling" parent	Physical abuse
	Parental neglect

*C. Black, 1981.
†S. Wegsheider, 1979.

The "Don't trust" rule stems directly from the inconsistent and unpredictable behaviors of family members. Neither the alcoholic nor the co-dependent parent can be depended on to listen to and respond sensitively to the children. The alcoholic parent lacks the ability to guide, model, focus on, nourish, and protect the child. As adults, these children of alcoholics often feel that they had no childhood and may have difficulty with self-nurturance or simply having fun.

The environment in an alcoholic home is often volatile and tense, offering arguments, battering, and tears in lieu of discussion and support. The inability to trust, like the verbal denial, is a characteristic that can endure well beyond the period of growing up in this toxic environment.

The "Don't feel" rule is learned through a lack of acknowledgment of the pain experienced by alcoholic family members living in this environment. For them, to feel is to experience pain. Anger is often bottled up and fermented into depression. Disappointment becomes twisted into blaming and guilt. Feeling helpless breeds shame and a feeling of being defective. Eventually, continued denial of the psychic pain can lead to losing touch with one's feelings altogether.

Several studies indicate that children of alcoholics are at high risk for hyperactivity, substance abuse, delinquency, truancy, cognitive impairment, social inadequacy, somatic problems, mood disorders, and physical abuse. These social difficulties set the children up for further rejection, reinforcing their poor sense of self-worth and inability to self-nurture. El-Guebaly and Offord (1977) state that emotional and behavioral problems are as much as six times higher in children of alcoholics than in children of non-substance-abusing parents.

Schafer's (1965) report adds that adolescents in alcoholic families feel lonely, isolated, and in need of reassurance, but lack the skills to satisfy their needs. Stuttering, fear of being alone, bedwetting, tantrums, and fighting with peers are also listed as potential side effects in these children. In addition to the psychological and emotional problems, maternal alcoholism during pregnancy can result in the physical and developmental impairments termed the fetal alcohol syndrome.

Studies have indicated that when they become adults, these unfortunate ones tend to find mates who perpetuate the same roles and dynamics of their family of origin, generation after generation. Black (1981) and Wegsheider (1979) describe the roles of the children in alcoholic families and how these roles are perpetuated in adult relationships.

The role that is regularly placed on the eldest (or only) child in the alcoholic family is that of the "responsible one" (Black) or "family hero" (Wegsheider). This is the parentified child who keeps everything under control and maintains the facade of "normality." This child is often a high achiever and a leader at school, and his or her parents are proud of the child's ability to take over. This is the child who as an adult becomes an ever-serious, rigid, and controlling "workaholic," and who has difficulty relaxing or having fun.

The "adjuster" (Black) or "lost child" (Wegsheider), often a second or middle child, is the flexible one who can adjust to any situation so long as he or she does not have to take responsibility for decision-making (which is the job of the responsible one). This child maintains a stance of helpless inability to make a difference. Rather than attempting to help others, the child masters the skill of diverting attention onto others. This child tries to be "invisible" in order to avoid pain. The stance of helplessness and the sense of a lack of control continue as the child grows into an overly dependent adult.

The "placater" (Black) or "mascot" (Wegsheider), sometimes the youngest child, is the one called on to settle disputes and to charm and console the family back to some semblance of peace. The placater does not disagree and is the first to apologize, even for things that are not his or her fault. This child who nurtures and "fixes" others may continue the role as a nurturing adult, such as a doctor, teacher, nurse, psychotherapist, or social worker. This "giver" will often find a mate who is a "taker," to balance the continuing relationship. The lack of support from an unavailable partner then perpetuates the dynamics of the family of origin.

The "acting-out child" (Black) or "scapegoat" (Wegsheider) is the one who does not distract attention from the family, but displays delinquent or problematic behavior, which serves to draw attention away from the alcoholic and on to the child as the "family problem." Because of poor self-esteem, self-blaming, and a feeling of inadequacy, the child's frustration and rage often carry over into antisocial adult behavior. Frequently, this child's behavior is what brings an alcoholic family to therapy, rather than the alcoholism itself.

ART THERAPY WITH ALCOHOLIC FAMILIES

A major difficulty in the treatment of a member from an alcoholic family, even long after the member is no longer with the family, is that denial is such an integral part of the family's interacting pattern that it continues in future relationships as well as in the therapy office. Damaged family members continue helplessly to perpetuate their unhealthy roles and poor communication patterns. Seldom is alcoholism presented as the "family problem"; instead, some member's behavior or mood disorder (usually resulting from this co-dependent's attempt to cope) is presented as the "identified patient's" symptom.

The value of art therapy as a treatment modality for alcoholic family members lies in its ability to access concealed or unconscious material through the use of metaphor and visual symbols. Once these are expressed in the concrete form of the art, the created product becomes a vehicle for breaking through the walls of denial.

Family dynamics and member roles can be clearly defined in the first one or two art therapy sessions through the use of a family collage and family drawings. The case example in this chapter demonstrates how the family's art productions illustrate family roles and patterns of interaction. The information revealed during the art production becomes, in turn, a basis for therapeutic intervention. The sense of safety through distancing is offered by use of the art object. Validation of individuals within a family is effected through the process of nonjudgmentally exploring and clarifying their art productions.

It is important to include here a comment on the therapist's style. When a therapist is overly confrontational early on in treatment, interpreting the images produced too soon, a family may show its disapproval by not attending the following session(s). Since the family productions are often full of potent imagery, there is a temptation for the therapist to move too quickly. By yielding to that temptation, the therapist risks losing the family prematurely, or at best having to deal with its reinforced defenses in response to the assault. The therapist may find it necessary continually to rejoin with the family ''power'' members in order to keep them in therapy.

Maximum benefit can be attained when a family is both in psychotherapy and attending support groups, such as AA, Alanon, ACOA, or other 12-Step programs. Even if the alcoholic refuses to attend AA or psychotherapy, the other family members can move toward healing through therapy. Despite the alcoholic's insistence on maintaining the illness, other family members do not have to continue their suffering in isolation.

Treatment Model

As with any family treatment, the primary goal is to assess the family and formulate a hypothesis about how the family ''symptom'' is maintained. When a family comes for treatment, most often a child is delegated the position of symptom-bearer for the family, manifested as some ''undesirable'' behavior. The person who brings the child for treatment most likely will be the ''power figure,'' who will play an important role in the family's staying in or leaving therapy, usually the ''enabling'' or co-dependent spouse. This is the person to whom the therapist must remain joined, in addition to the ''patient,'' in order to keep the family coming to therapy.

A combination of psychodynamic, communication, and structural theories can be useful for intervention in working with these families. Since mixed and unclear communication is a trait of alcoholic families, it is particularly important for the therapist to insist on clarity when the family members discuss their experiences and work.

A logical beginning is to request individual members to draw a picture of the family problem. Upon completing the drawings, the members are asked individually about their productions. If at least three family members are present, it is helpful to follow the first process with circular questioning (of one member about the behaviors between two others) to obtain diagnostic information about the family dynamics. Inquiry is made about what has been done to deal with the problem and how successful it was. The family members can then be given a directive to draw or to create a collage about how they expect therapy to change the symptom. Similarities and differences can be discussed and a treatment goal established.

The next step is to explore the individual family roles. This may be accomplished by using any or all of three directives.

The individuals are requested to choose one or two collage pictures that tell something about themselves. They then place their pictures on a single, large sheet of paper in any order they choose. The therapist pays particular attention to the order of who goes before whom and picture placement (who is next to whom). The members are requested to describe the images they chose, and then to discuss what they noticed about the order and placement. The therapist can add information or ask for clarity, if appropriate.

The second directive involves a nonverbal conjoint family drawing. In this process the family is requested to draw together on the page without talking and to put down their pens when finished. Again, discussion follows about how and where members chose to represent themselves and the order of the art process. The therapist asks if there were any broken rules, such as changing color or talking during the drawing. In the verbal family drawing, the only difference is the freedom to talk during the drawing. Differences in how the members behaved and experienced the first and second drawings can be discussed.

"Free drawings" are drawings that are spontaneously produced by a client during a session, as opposed to a drawing produced in response to a directive from the therapist. Potent imagery often emerges within these free drawings, which can express a concealed response to whatever is being overtly discussed in the session. These images can make a powerful statement about that client's experience within the family and attitude toward the therapy itself. With individual members of an alcoholic family, nondirective art of all types can offer a wealth of diagnostic information and a source for healing. Remaining within whatever metaphor is expressed in the art, rather than interpreting it in relation to life experience, helps to maintain the safety of "distance." In this way, the client may be willing to delve more deeply into the meaning of the work without feeling threatened.

Since the symptom-bearing member often suffers from poor self-esteem, low self-confidence, and a feeling of powerlessness, building up these areas is an underlying issue to be kept in mind. The unconditional acceptance of whatever art is produced by the client and careful storage of the products make a statement about the client's worth. Processing the art productions through discussion provides the therapist with opportunities to focus on the client's strengths, normalizing and accepting whatever feelings emerge during that process.

Clinical Example

Thirteen-year-old Jim McKee was the youngest of five children and the identified patient in this Caucasian family. His symptoms included truancy, oppositional behavior, running away for short periods, and temper tantrums. Despite Mrs. McKee's (personal) diagnosis of Jim's having an attention deficit/hyperactivity disorder (ADHD), he remained seated, still, and focused throughout sessions. If anything, Jim's quiet withdrawal, downcast eyes, and sighs were more characteristic of depression than of hyperactivity.

Although Jim's father was an active alcoholic, he did not believe that he had a "drinking problem." Mr. McKee was quite intelligent, but his unpredictable and inconsistent behavior created difficulty both at home and in his maintaining regular appointments. Mrs. McKee presented as a caring, concerned woman but exhibited symptoms of a histrionic personality disorder and of moderately severe depression. She stated that although Mr. McKee's behavior when drinking was disruptive to their family life, she intended to stay with him "for better or worse." Her co-dependent role can be seen clearly throughout the art she produced.

Mrs. McKee appeared to have a poor sense of boundaries and often acted in an invasive and overcontrolling manner with her children. She needed continual reassurance and attention. She admitted that when she reached her tolerance level of being "ignored," she threw a tantrum, screaming out in rage at the children. To Mr. McKee, she spoke quietly and with deference during sessions.

In addition to her predetermined diagnosis of Jim, Mrs. McKee also described her daughter, 16-year-old Madonna, as hyperactive. During sessions, Madonna often daydreamed, and moved and spoke in a rather lethargic manner. The only times she appeared animated were when she was arguing with her mother, having a tantrum, or weeping. Perhaps what her mother perceived as hyperactivity was, in fact, the irritability common in dysthymia. Nevertheless, pursuing her assessment of Jim's and Madonna's symptoms, Mrs. McKee insisted on medication and/or treatment based on her personal diagnoses. She seldom informed the children of the purpose of their visits to doctors or of medications prescribed until after they had already been administered. In this manner, she avoided responding to the children's confrontations or refusal to be treated.

The two oldest McKee children, Patrick and Junior, lived outside the home.

The middle child and only female sibling, Madonna, was under treatment in the same clinic as Jim for her chronic depression. Like her mother, she had a poor sense of boundaries and was easily influenced by others' opinions. She and her mother regularly engaged in loud disagreements, which escalated to screaming matches.

The fourth child, Robin (15), seemed to play the role of family hero. Popular with his peers, Robin was also looked up to by Jim, Madonna, and even Mrs. McKee for decision-making and "running" the family in Mr. McKee's absence. Robin and Madonna were quite close and usually excluded Jim from their relationship, either by ignoring him or by calling him and his behavior "stupid." Jim appeared to be envious of Robin's status and attempted to imitate his brother, for which the family berated him. When Jim felt "ganged up on" by family criticism, his solution was to remain silent, keeping his accumulating rage to himself. His silence also proved to be useful in manipulating his family.

According to his chart, Jim McKee's oppositional behavior at home had not improved after two years of group therapy. Although his group therapist stated that Jim's behavior during sessions had improved substantially, Mrs. McKee complained that he was often truant from school and continually defied her. When Jim did not wish to comply with his mother's wishes, he would either throw a temper tantrum or run away and hide from her. During Jim's tantrums, Mrs. McKee often would literally sit on him to keep him from hurting himself or destroying things.

Jim's group therapy leader requested that Jim receive individual counseling. Keeping in mind that Jim's problem behavior was predominantly related to home environment, I recommended family art therapy as a treatment approach.

In my first meeting with this family, Mrs. McKee accompanied Jim to the session. After introducing myself and asking if they had any questions, I asked Jim and Mrs. McKee to draw what each considered to be the family problem that brought them to therapy. Jim drew a witchlike woman yelling at two children. He explained that it was a picture of his mother screaming at a friend of Jim's for borrowing something without asking. Jim stated that his mother was always yelling. Mrs. McKee responded with silence to Jim's statement.

Mrs. McKee drew Figure 4.1, which shows all the family members. In the drawing, she shows Mr. McKee holding his bottle, smiling and oblivious

Figure 4.1. Meeting the family.

to her. She drew herself with one hand raised, perhaps in confusion or in aggression against Mr. McKee. Further confusion is indicated by the presence of a smiling sun with rain (a double message). The five smiling children are shown in the foreground, forming a barricade that blocks the broken pathway to the house. The lack of downstairs windows, the incomplete door, the broken path, and the ''barricade'' together implied a family well defended against intrusion. The three flowers and three clouds may symbolize the three children left to nurture themselves in a home that lacks a strong parental subsystem. Her drawings of the children are not as complete as those for the parents, reflecting the mother's co-dependent focus on her husband to the exclusion of the children. The children are shown in order of age (and with decreasing detail), from Patrick on the left to Jim on the right. Mrs. McKee stated that her husband's drinking was the family problem. Although Jim (and not her husband) was presented as the ''identified patient,'' Mrs. McKee did not connect her husband's alcoholism to Jim's behavior.

Jim said few words during the first session, often answering with a shrug of his shoulders or a single word. Mrs. McKee often spoke for him, signaling her enmeshment.

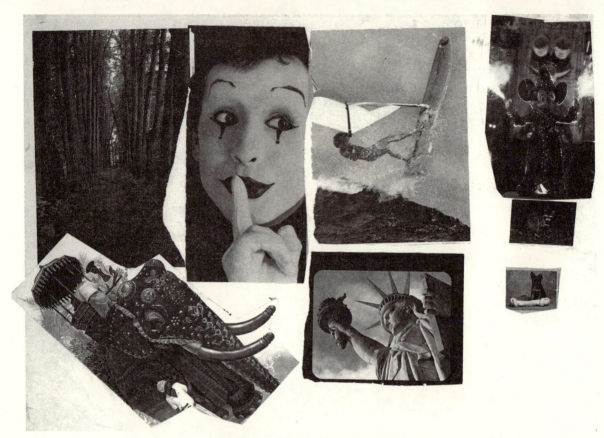

Figure 4.2. A family collage.

In order to assess the family dynamics further, I requested that all family members be present at the second session. Mrs. McKee protested that her husband would not attend, but she promised to try to persuade him to do so.

Both parents and the three children living at home arrived for the next session. I invited the family to introduce themselves by choosing collage pictures that said something about them, and to place the pictures together on a large sheet of paper in any order they wished. This directive was chosen as a way of obtaining diagnostic material to define the family's dynamics and alliances. Figure 4.2 shows their response. After they had completed their collage, the imagery was discussed.

Mr. McKee was the first to place his picture, in the upper left-hand corner. The picture showed a serene and isolated tree-lined path leading to a cathedral-like arch and crossed trees. Two smaller trees form a block to the path's end. He stated that it looked like a ''nice place to be.'' I empathized that it can be difficult to find a quiet, isolated spot in a house full of teenagers. Mrs. McKee snickered, but made no comment until I asked what was amusing her. She stated that Mr. McKee was seldom around the house; he was usually off ''somewhere else.''

Following Mr. McKee, Robin placed his pictures adjacent to his father's. Commenting on his mime, who appeared to be warning the audience to be quiet, Robin stated that he would like to be an actor. Based on the Black (1981) and Wegsheider (1979) models, I wondered if Robin was the "family hero," whose job it was to keep everything looking good. In that role, Robin would already be an "actor." His image of the off-balance surfer was explained as his desire to learn this sport. In future sessions, the image of the off-balance or potentially endangered skateboarder or surfer would be repeated by both Robin and Jim, perhaps reflecting the precarious and often volatile environment at home.

Jim then placed his pictures in the upper right, next to Robin's. He stated that the Mickey Mouse figure in the "Sorcerer's Apprentice" costume represented his enjoyment of playing tricks on people. When I asked Jim if he was familiar with this Disney animated feature, he nodded. I then asked if he remembered how Mickey's trick had backfired and gotten him into trouble. Jim first looked blank and then quickly changed the focus to his raccoon picture, stating that raccoons are smart. I agreed, adding that they are also very clean animals that bravely defended their families. I then stated that it is unfortunate that such smart animals were often blamed for getting into people's trash and making messes. Although Jim did not respond, Madonna said emphatically that she was always angry with him for getting into her things. Robin supported Madonna's comment by stating that Jim regularly took his clothes. I hypothesized that Jim was delegated the role of "acting-out child/scapegoat." As stated above, this is not an uncommon role for the identified patient.

Mrs. McKee's elegantly dressed elephant could have been placed upright under Jim's pictures. Instead, she chose to put her picture at an off-balance angle, blocking the path of Mr. McKee's "spot" and turning it into a trap. This may have demonstrated her desire to have more control over her aloof husband, which, in turn, threw her parental role "off balance." She referred to the ornamentation as reflecting her enjoyment of dressing up in costumes to perform liturgical dances and her wish to be pampered like the elephant.

Mrs. McKee said that her Statue of Liberty stood for her wish to be freer of obligations at home. This liberty image was repeated in the family drawings that followed. Mrs. McKee later revealed that she spent much of her time taking her children to various Alateen meetings and to therapy, as well as in keeping notebooks on each child's behavior for the "Because I Love You" meetings. I complimented Mrs. McKee on her dedication and "stored" the information for a future intervention.

Finally, Madonna placed her needy puppy with the huge bone in the only available space, with a margin bordering all sides. She stated simply that the picture was "cute." Although the picture was quite small, the space framing it served to draw attention to the small image. I wondered if Madonna's role was that of ''lost child/adjuster.'' She was easily influenced by and overly sensitive to peers, modeling after her mother's emotionality and poor sense of boundaries. Her struggle with individuation was reflected in the space surrounding her picture.

Following the collage discussion, I asked the McKees to do a nonverbal drawing in which each member would retain the same marker color throughout the drawing. Members were to signal that they were finished by putting their pens down. The drawing in Figure 4.3 is the result; it repeats many of the traits seen in Figure 4.2.

As the drawing began, Jim produced his green surfer in the upper left as Mrs. McKee drew her orange sun on the upper right. Mrs. McKee repeated this sun image (with a star on its forehead) in several of her drawings, although usually with the eyes open. As the drawing progressed, Mrs. McKee intrusively drew her hearts and flowers into everyone else's ''space,'' again reflecting her loose boundaries. She placed a dancing female figure in the middle of the page, pursued by a male figure that resembled the one for her oldest child, Patrick, in Figure 4.1. She hummed as she drew, first placing an arm around Robin, then around Jim. She whispered a request for Jim to put a stem and leaves (support) under her flowers. Her sun and female faces have closed eyes, perhaps expressing the denial of the family's dysfunction. Despite the ''loving'' gestures, none of her figures are touching. The disconnected line between the bottom figures and the rest of the drawing may show her desire for a closer alliance with her husband, although Madonna's black dots intrude on the space.

In Jim's drawing on the upper left, he shows himself as a heroic and muscular surfer who is rescuing the rest of the family from an overturned, disjointed surfboard. Jim portrayed his desire to be more like Robin (the family hero). The other members look as if they were left ''hanging,'' particularly with the ominous sharklike fin of the surfboard protruding upward. (The shark image was repeated later in several of Jim's art products.) Jim's surfer greets his oldest brother in the jet. A ''girl'' watches from the shore near a fruit-bearing tree with a weak trunk, observing the family from a distance. This figure may represent the therapist. Jim's thin flower stems look inadequate to hold up the mother's large blossoms. Jim also used his green to color in the star on the sun.

Robin added to the drawing by completing a separate rendition of the family, titling it the ''happy family together'' (lower right). He placed a boundary line around his drawing. I noticed that in Robin's drawing the two brothers who did not live in the family home were shown apart from the group. It is also interesting to note that his image of the mother is placed between the younger brothers, while the drawing of Madonna is placed next

Figure 4.3. A "nonverbal" family drawing.

to the father. I noted alliances and wondered about the possibility of incest. Robin's drawing of his father is the only one in which the eyes are unfocused, perhaps portraying intoxication. The unsmiling figure drawn by Madonna looks confused.

Madonna, using black, drew her numerously petaled, tightly controlled flower on the right, with another flower next to but not touching Robin's outline. The second flower has a womblike or possibly a phallic/testicular form, again triggering my curiosity about Madonna's sexuality.

As his family drew, Mr. McKee remained seated and watched them. When all of the others had finished, Mr. McKee used red to create his "duck" in about 10 seconds, then sat down again. His duck was created from a cursive S, to which he added wings, eye, and beak. He stated that he had been drawing the same duck for 45 years and that was all he ever drew, echoing his resistance to change.

During their discussion, the family was able to identify the order of the drawing. When I asked about which things members noticed, all three children said that Mrs. McKee had broken the "no-talking" rule. Although she looked a little surprised and embarrassed at the confrontation, she was also smiling. She had already stated that the only time she was noticed at home was when she yelled (acted out).

In the last drawing of the session (Figure 4.4), the family members were requested to create a verbal family drawing, still using one color throughout. In an effort to learn more about the father's relationships with the other family members, I requested Mr. McKee to be the "boss" of this drawing, telling each person when to draw and where. Resisting the directive in spite of my reminders, Mr. McKee asked the boys if they wanted a turn, then asked Madonna, and finally Mrs. McKee. He offered no instruction during the drawing, but merely watched. His inability or refusal to instruct demonstrates his unavailability as a parent in the home.

In this drawing, Jim repeated his surfing hero, except that he wrote "me . . . me." In addition to using a different color (dark blue), Jim included some new details. The surfer, instead of smiling, is now yelling from atop the smaller surfboard that is completely out of the water. The surfer's torso

Figure 4.4.   A "verbal" family drawing.

has more detail and he looks as if he is about to be enveloped by the pointed wave. A more asexual and aggressive looking "girl" stands on a rock island next to the fruitless tree, which now has a stronger trunk but is no longer supported by the ground. The heart drawn between the figures was drawn this time by Jim (rather than Mrs. McKee) and filled in by Madonna. This time, Junior was eliminated from the family imagery.

Jim's poignant attempts to draw attention to himself may indicate his discomfort with the information revealed through his family's imagery.

Using gray, Madonna drew a female figure with highly emphasized hair (associated with active fantasy). Her person is smoking a cigarette, again reflecting oral needs (like the puppy) and her aggression. Although the figure is wearing a dress, female sexual features are absent. The tightly clasped hands, rigid posture, and sideways glancing eyes reflect her discomfort, and perhaps a fear of getting "out of control" by revealing too much. Her dividing groundline appears to press down on Jim's drawing. Jim ignored the division and intrusively drew his phallic-looking jet over Madonna's figure's legs and pelvic area. A very small stick figure appears to flee from the larger female.

Also using blue, Robin drew a skateboarder performing a precarious jump. Despite cheers from the onlookers, the skater looks out of control, ready to fall. The hair on the skater resembles Robin's self-portrait from the previous drawing.

Mrs. McKee drew herself performing a liturgical dance. Again, her eyes are closed; this time she has no feet (reflecting her feeling of powerless immobility). The figure resembles her liberty image from Figure 4.2. She includes the circled pentagram, a symbol often used in occult practices. In contrast with the previous drawing, this time Mrs. McKee created a more substantial figure, which stayed mostly in her own space.

Again, Mr. McKee waited until all were finished, then drew his 10-second red duck. As the directive and drawing were discussed, I remarked that Mr. McKee gave only a small amount of instruction as "boss" and asked if he usually did not exert a lot of authority at home. He responded that he would rather allow the others to "do their own thing." I wondered whether the children's acting out at home was a way of determining where those unclear limits were. In a later session, the family members were unable to define clearly any house "rules."

All the family members were requested to return the following week for another family session. Mr. McKee stated emphatically that they would all attend.

Following the present session, I was concerned that I had moved too fast and that the abundance of material that was revealed in one session might be overwhelming for the family. Either the concern was valid or perhaps the family was simply manifesting its inconsistency, since only the mother attended the next session.

Mrs. McKee revealed her own inability to set limits for or to exert authority over her children by stating that she was often unable to get her children to their sessions regularly. As in most of the sessions, Mrs. McKee looked tired and depressed; she had difficulty staying focused on the discussion.

I took advantage of the situation to explore Mrs. McKee's background and current goals. She revealed in drawings that she had been the abused and neglected child of an alcoholic mother on whom she could not depend for security. In marrying an unavailable and inconsistent husband, she had continued the dynamic. She explained that the only way she earned attention from the other members was when she had a temper tantrum, which she called a "nervous breakdown." Although she felt deprived, her poor sense of self-worth and lack of entitlement induced Mrs. McKee to focus her attention on other family members. She tended to keep her frustration inside until it reached explosive proportions; then she would scream at whoever happened to be with her (usually Jim or Madonna).

When I asked if Mrs. McKee had considered getting some psychotherapy to help with her difficulties, she responded that she had tried three different 12-Step programs, as well as "Because I Love You" meetings for parents of hyperactive and acting-out children. I recommended that she supplement her group meetings with individual therapy, which she agreed would be helpful.

Near the end of her session, Mrs. McKee stated that although Jim was waiting in the car, she had been unable to convince him to come in. Up until this time, she had (by omission) implied that she had come alone. I wondered if Mrs. McKee wanted therapy for herself, but, because of her lack of entitlement, was unable to offer it to herself without an excuse (such as that which a poorly attended family session would offer). Allowing Jim to refuse attendance had also allowed Mrs. McKee to have an individual therapy session.

This pattern occurred several times throughout the therapy. Attendance was inconsistent from one week to the next, often including one parent and one child, or two children, or just Mrs. McKee. Mrs. McKee stated that she simply did not have the energy to gather the resistant members for sessions. Mr. McKee saw no benefit in family (or any other) psychotherapy, and so offered little support. Throughout therapy, "forgetting" to relay messages, and mixed and double meanings proved to be the expected form of communication with the McKee's.

At the next session, Mrs. McKee arrived with only Jim. It appeared that

Mr. McKee's lack of attendance may have been his attempt to avoid dealing with the effect he had on his children and his role in their difficulties.

I asked Jim and Mrs. McKee to each create a collage about how having the entire family present was different from having just the two of them. They were requested to include a title or a few words next to each picture, explaining what it was about.

In discussing their work, Jim stated that he thought the instruction had been to make a collage about anything he liked (resisting the directive). This "not hearing" proved to be part of the poor communication pattern, as well as contributing to Jim's power within the family.

In Jim's collage (not shown), he chose the following images, which were carefully placed in a symmetrical pattern around the page. In the upper left is a large picture of an eclipse with a flare exploding from behind the shadow that does not quite hide the brightness. Indeed, the eclipsed power he experienced in this alcoholic home eventually accumulated to an explosive level. I wondered if this image was representative of Jim's (and his mother's) temper tantrums. Beneath the eclipsed sun is an illustration of a two-story wooden house on the edge of a lake, with trees in the background. A ramp leads from the quiet house to a dock, on which rest two wind-surfing boards. Although there are life jackets next to the surfboards, they are not being used and no people are present. It appears that the only access to the house is either from the dock (by boat) or by tramping through the brush to the back. Despite all the reflecting windows, the house appears to be isolated and well protected from intrusion.

On the right of his collage, Jim placed a futuristic picture of alien men with jet-powered seats being dropped from parachutes, intermixed with a jet, all moving in a circular pattern. The overall effect is one of precarious confusion and danger. In the lower right, he placed a cartoon of a distraught Russian in a fallout shelter, sitting at a table with a bottle of vodka, a candle, and a tiny flag. The Russian's distress comes from three bombs that are determinedly pushing their way through the ground toward the shelter. Jim stated that the bombs had backfired by aiming at the person who had set them off (which reminded me of Jim's sorcerer's apprentice, Mickey, and the magic that backfired).

In the center, Jim placed two images. The top image shows a surreal world over a form that looks like blue liquid, much like photographs of milk drops taken with fast-speed film. It looks as if the world is raised up only momentarily for observation before it plunges back into the liquid (like the elusive family members who will not consistently attend). Although a source of light is implied, the background is dark and dusklike. The lower image is of a red-helmeted driver and snowmobile streaking by as if racing, another indication of speed, potential danger, and short-term observation. I believe that Jim had dealt with the directive after all, as well as his reaction to the previous week's fast pace and overwhelming information.

Mrs. McKee created the collage shown in Figure 4.5. Beginning in the upper left, she shows her identity confusion. Despite her stated pride in being part American Indian, her facial features reflect her other ethnicity. The picture is a cartoon of a woman "riding the fence" between AA and ACOA. As discussed earlier, Mrs. McKee had difficulty deciding just which 12-step program she should attend. Moving to the right, she showed her husband, "drinking, and can't see life clearly . . . that he's hurting his family because of it. He's all fogged up in mind and vision." I noticed that in the photograph the person handing the man a drink is a woman, signaling the co-dependence. On the right, Mrs. McKee shows both her intrusiveness and her difficulty in paying attention to her children's attempts at setting boundaries in her selection of the picture showing a boy with a bitten apple in his hands while a little girl puts yet a fourth apple to the boy's mouth. Jim responded by stating that he disliked the "health foods" that his mother continually attempted to force on the family. In the lower right, an older

Figure 4.5. Mrs. McKee shows her roles in the family.

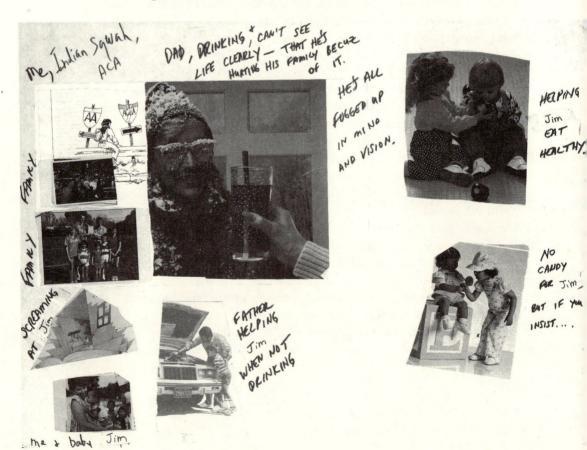

child is taking candy from a younger one, showing Mrs. McKee's experience of helplessness in influencing and setting limits in her family.

In the lower center, Mrs. McKee placed her image of a man teaching a boy about car repair. She stated that when Mr. McKee was not out drunk, he took time to do things with Jim. When I asked if he enjoyed doing things with his father, Jim said "Yes," but with little enthusiasm. I suggested that perhaps Jim would like to share a session with his father; Mrs. McKee said excitedly that would be "a good idea." Jim was noncommittal, but agreed to invite his father to attend.

In the lower left, Mrs. McKee placed her photo of a mother and baby, along with a cartoon of a woman rushing out, dragging along a child. She admitted that she often treated Jim as though he were much younger than his 13 years ("around nine") and was always screaming at him to go to his sessions when he resisted. Finally, on the center left, there are two pictures, each titled "family." In the top, smaller picture, a grandmother, parents, and five children are shown, huddled together against the cold night, but smiling. This image portrays a collusion in denial of the discomfort, for the sake of the photograph. In the larger picture, rather than a family, five young soccer players stand with two men holding a plaque. Mrs. McKee was surprised to notice that this was not a picture of a family, and indeed lacked women (mother) altogether. Perhaps she was treated more like one of the children in this "team" (family) than a parent, while Robin acted as a parentified child.

To further assess the relationship between Jim and his mother, I requested that they do a nonverbal dual drawing in which each retained one marker color throughout. Jim used green and his mother used brown. His mother's attempts to control Jim are again clear in this drawing, shown in Figure 4.6. Mrs. McKee produced a drawing showing one of Jim's experiences in school, in which he was treated unfairly by a teacher. She complimented Jim's choosing to ignore the situation, rather than to stand up for his rights, stating that it was better than making a scene (passively submitting). Since she was unsure of which class it had been and the exact circumstances, she asked Jim. Jim's smiling face on the front desk indicated his presence and that the story was his to tell (not hers).

On the left side, Jim drew a tall, pointed mountain and placed a sure-footed goat atop the precipice. I wondered if Jim was willing to risk a precarious situation in order to escape his mother's intrusion. Mrs. McKee drew a flower at the base of the hills, then followed the goat's upward trail, and finally created stars and moon for the goat to gaze at. After several incorrect guesses, Mrs. McKee wrote "5th" at the base to indicate the class in which Jim's story took place. (I recalled that Jim was the 5th child, and also that a "5th" is a way of describing a bottle of liquor.) Jim playfully

Figure 4.6. A "dual drawing" reflects enmeshment between mother and son.

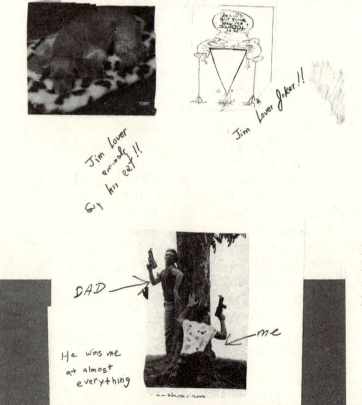

Figure 4.7.
Father and son drawings show the son's double-bind position.

transformed the "5th" into a man with a hat. Mrs. McKee included herself by drawing a taller female next to Jim's figure. Jim added some "flowers" in the hand of his figure, offering them to the female.

In the discussion that followed, it was noticed once again that Mrs. McKee ignored "rules" by talking during the drawing. I found that "not following the rules" was a frequent pattern in the mother's behavior. While inquiring about Mrs. McKee's drawing into Jim's "space," I empathized that it can be particularly difficult for a mother to allow her youngest child to grow up and separate. I interpreted Jim's mountain goat as his declaration of a desire for independence.

At the end of the session, it was agreed that Mr. McKee would be invited to attend the next meeting. The following week, Mr. McKee accompanied Jim, while Mrs. McKee declined, having "other things to do."

After I informed Mr. McKee of how, in the previous week, Jim had stated that he enjoyed doing things with his father, Mr. McKee looked surprised and mildly pleased. (In most sessions, Mr. McKee seldom showed any affect other than a yawn of boredom.) In an effort to raise Jim's self-esteem and explore his relationship with his father, I asked them to create collages about what characteristics each liked in the other. Figure 4.7 shows their two collages.

Mr. McKee placed two pictures on the left half of the page. Under the resting dog, he wrote, "Jim loves animals, esp. his cat!!" (Note, there were pictures of cats in the collage supplies.) Mr. McKee stated that although Jim liked his cat, sometimes he treated it too roughly, thereby adding a barb to his compliment. In the middle, cartoon characters declare, "Junior's not doing well in school, is he???" In the cartoon, a couple with bared teeth, pointing at each other, create two angles of a triangle, whose third point aims at the child beneath them. Mr. McKee titled this cartoon, "Jim loves jokes!!" and connected the cartoon to his son, Junior, who is "not doing well." While Jim admitted that he enjoyed playing jokes and tricks on others, this cartoon reminded me of the backfiring effect in Jim's other collages and how parental conflict can manifest in children's symptoms. Mixed and double messages are clearly shown. When questioned about the confusion, Mr. McKee shrugged it off as unimportant and meaningless.

In Jim's collage, he stated that although he liked to play games with this father, "He wins me at almost everything." Jim's picture shows two young men who have been playing the game "splat gun" with paint bullets. The one crouching down has obviously been shot several times from behind, and is looking in the wrong direction for his opponent. The standing man sneaks around the tree for another ambush from behind. The collage shows Jim in the no-win situation of either losing or not playing (abandonment).

This was the first of three father and son sessions. At the next session, the topic arose of Jim's difficulty with his math class and teacher, who, he said, treated him unfairly. Jim was often disciplined for disrupting the class with talking and jokes. Within the one session, Mr. McKee gave the following advice at different times: (1) "Stop talking so much." (2) "Speak up; stand up for yourself." (3) "Lay low and ignore it." The mixed advice left Jim unsure about whether he was to speak up or stay quiet. Whenever these double messages were interpreted to the family, the children would often respond first with a surprised look and then with silence.

During the discussion, Jim created the undirected (free) drawing in Figure 4.8. In this drawing, Jim shows himself metaphorically as the family scapegoat, deflecting attention from the dysfunction. I asked Jim what his figures would say if they could speak. His central male with a "screwdriver" wound in his large nose exclaims, "LOOK AT ME!!" as a tiny doctor points and answers, "OK." Jim stated that, on the lower left, the little female figure's large hand is full of screwdrivers as she curses at the flying kite that appears to be wedged into the corner. The female figure may have represented the volatile mother trying to capture the kite (her husband), which is flying off.

The wedged kite reminded me of how, in their first collage, Mrs. McKee had turned Mr. McKee's isolated spot into a trap. Anyone who attempted to get the female's attention while she was focused on the kite would risk injury from the screwdrivers. Jim's drawing seems to reflect the centricity of the father's alcoholism and the resulting damage to the children. The tiny helping figure would be limited in dealing with such a serious wound, perhaps showing Jim's lack of confidence in therapy's ability to make any significant difference.

In a later session, although all members were requested to attend, only Mr. and Mrs. McKee arrived with Jim. Mr. McKee sat down mumbling about his "rotten kids" who never listen, and how they would all be better off if the children were put into foster care and he was rid of them. When asked if he was serious about this, Mr. McKee mumbled, "Yeah" as his wife sat looking tired and depressed.

The plasticene had already been set out and Jim modeled a black pistol as his father was talking about "kicking the children out." I inquired about Jim's experience of what it felt like to listen to his father saying these things. Jim answered in an almost inaudible whisper, "Mad." I then asked Mrs. McKee if she had heard Jim's response and she answered, "Jim never talks." When requested to repeat his answer so that it could be heard, Jim did so. At that point, I stated that perhaps what seemed like Jim's "never talking" was instead his not being heard. The family was then asked to make something together from the plasticene.

After some planning about what to create, the family decided to make fruit. While Jim and his father tended to make more common fruits, such

Figure 4.8. Jim shows himself the family scapegoat.

as orange and banana, Mrs. McKee molded more exotic examples. This difference seemed to concretely represent stylistic differences in their personalities. The conflicts over Mrs. McKee's attempts to control the family diet became clear when Mr. McKee molded some cookies and candy for the collection as Mrs. McKee molded tiny vitamin pills. Mr. McKee referred to his wife's cooking as "disaster number three," and so on. Jim then created a bowl to hold the fruit, possibly signifying his desire to keep the family together. Finally, Mr. McKee molded handles for the bowl, showing his attempt to contain and control the family. When their work was completed, I asked the family to choose a title for it. The final decision rested with Jim, who chose, "Foods for Life." The family's tension level had lowered considerably compared with that on their arrival.

The plasticene works produced by this family did not fare well in the trunk of a hot car, and so could not be shown here. This is particularly unfortunate, since plasticene in combination with small figures proved to be one of Jim's more significant and powerful media.

At a later family session, the members were requested to draw about a family problem that they would like to resolve through therapy, and how they would like that situation to be different. All three children made drawings of their mother's yelling too much. Robin's drawing also complained that the family did not do things together and that Mrs. McKee was seldom around to cook or help with the house. Mrs. McKee's drawing complained that she was always listening for her absent children, while feeling that she was never heard. Evidently, the children would tire of the yelling and either ignore their mother or simply leave. She would have to have one of her "breakdowns" in order to get any attention. Following one of her tantrums, the children would behave well for a few days, reinforcing for her the effectiveness of her tantrum. In another session with Mrs. McKee, I paradoxically described her tantrum and notebook keeping as "giving too much attention to the children," and suggested that she pay more attention to Mr. McKee so he would not feel "left out."

As usual, Mr. McKee used his own pen from his pocket rather than my materials. He complained that the children did not follow the few rules the family had. However, when asked to define those rules, family members were unable to give definitive answers. I suggested that perhaps the rules were not clear and could be better defined. As a homework assignment, they were asked to list which rules each thought was important to the family. Predictably, by the next meeting, no one had completed, or even remembered, the assignment.

During the session, the family revealed that a certain sequence occurred repeatedly between Jim and his brother Robin. Jim would tease his older brother or take something that belonged to him. Robin would warn Jim to stop, "or else," and the two would begin to wrestle in fun, which would escalate to fighting. Since he was bigger and stronger than Jim, Robin would usually get the upper hand and Jim would then get a weapon in order to avoid losing. In one such incident, Jim had nicked Robin's hand with a knife. Mrs. McKee stated that if Mr. McKee were home, he would break up the fight. However, if Mrs. McKee were home, she would refuse to become involved, going to another room and shutting herself away from the boys. She felt that she had neither the energy nor enough influence to intervene.

In his individual sessions, Jim would often create large collages with overlapping images showing potential danger, collisions, and so on, and then would give these collages benign titles. An example is a collage to which he kept adding until he had three large pages taped together. His collage included people about to be attacked by sharks, a basketball player about to be overcome by a tidal wave, a soldier's hand raised as if swimming through the muck, a surfer placed on his side, and a cartoon of an out-of-control heavy-metal performer next to a rifle aimed at an attacking shark. A cartoon of Snoopy dressed as a detective was placed next to the surfer, perhaps representing me. His title for the collage was simply, "The Beach."

In one of Jim's plasticene creations, dinosaurs fight next to a volcano that is about to erupt. Two "parent" gorillas on another island are unable to get the young dinosaurs' attention in order to stop the fight or warn of the dangerous volcano. In another plasticene work, Jim showed cowboys and Indians, as well as their animal companions, fighting. (I remembered that the mother professed to be part Indian.) He described that at the end of the fight only two cowboys were left, to which Jim added clay details in order to represent himself and his father. Jim was clearly depicting the volatile situation at home.

I requested a meeting of all family members in order to get a clearer picture of the fighting between Jim and Robin and to assess whether the situation was reportable. I emphasized that it was necessary for Robin to represent himself in the discussion.

When the family members arrived, I reminded them of the purpose of the session. Circular-style questioning was accomplished through the art by having each member create a collage about how the fights got started, escalated, and were resolved. Figure 4.9 of the mother's collage shows themes present in the others' collages as well.

In Mrs. McKee's collage (Figure 4.9), on the left, she shows two boys teasing, one by cutting off the hair of the other, while both smile. Beneath that, placed on its side, is a picture of two baseball players enthusiastically embracing after a victory. The players are about the same size, as are Jim and Robin despite two years difference in age. She stated that these two stood for her sons' close times, compared to their times of conflict.

On the top, Mrs. McKee gives a title of ''War'' to two of the pictures, which show double messages. In the center, a sportsman seen from behind is holding a rifle. He wears a cap much like a cap often worn by Mr. McKee. He is seen from the back (unaware of the ''audience''). On the right, a bedraggled soldier smiles as he holds a walkie-talkie (a communication tool rather than a weapon). These seem more accurately to reflect the relationship

Figure 4.9. The ''war'' between Jim and Robin.

between the parents than between the boys, since Mrs. McKee is weary from her futile attempts to communicate with her husband.

On the bottom, she overlapped three pictures of men in lab coats with various telephones in their laps. The figures pose as "See no evil, speak no evil, hear no evil." The telephones (as instruments of communication) are in direct contrast to the poses of refusal to hear, see, or speak. Mrs. McKee said that when the boys fought she went into her room and closed the door in order to avoid getting involved. She stated that she was too tired to intervene and often expected Mr. McKee to rescue her from that role. Her collage clearly shows her denial about the meaning and seriousness of the boys' fighting.

Usually a prolific artist during the sessions, Robin produced two drawings in addition to the collage portraying his fights with Jim. In his first pencil drawing, Robin drew Jim defying orders to take out the trash or stop teasing. In two of the three scenes on this page, Robin drew himself as muscle-bound but headless, as if their bodies functioned without thought in a predestined role. In one of the scenes, Jim has no head, while in the other he has been knocked unconscious by Robin (X's for eyes). In the third scene (same drawing), Robin's bodiless head screams as knives representing Jim point toward him.

Robin's collage shows the three steps in the fight sequence: the teasing or mimicking, the fight, and the resolution by Jim's either crying for help or getting some weapon. In the first picture, one figure (Jim) follows in the footsteps of another (to tease Robin). The picture below it shows a soldier shooting a bazooka from behind sandbags (to represent the fight). The third is an illustration of a weeping figure in the foreground as figures with backs turned stand with umbrellas in the background, unaware of the misery of the figure they do not see. Robin stated that the picture shows how Jim cries when Robin gets the better of him. The collage echoes the parents' indifference and resistance to acknowledging their children's suffering, shielding themselves through isolation. Robin's third picture was created after his father's collage. It shows a large figure (Jim) about to step on a tiny one (Robin), and explains that Jim would like to be the stronger one of the two in order to "beat up" Robin (or avoid being hurt).

Madonna refused to make a collage, explaining that she was not present to see the fight. Although I suggested that she may have had some ideas about how the fights usually occurred, she still resisted, stating flatly that the boys were "just messing around" and not really fighting.

Jim's collage, titled "The Big Fight," shows a combination of fighting and friendship, as do both parents' collages. In it, one of the pictures is of two adult twins smiling at each other. A lasso that encircles the two is connected above their heads to a photo of them as children grimacing at each other, contradicting the smiles. Denial of true feeling is again revealed. Beneath this is an illustration of a frowning devil child and two fighting robots. To the left, and taking up most of the page, is a mildly smiling young soldier and the American eagle insignia. This passively smiling soldier reminded me of the headless fighting figures from Robin's drawing, performing a function without questioning.

At the top of Mr. McKee's collage, a man using weights bears the title, "Robin, mucho macho," defining Robin's attitude. Under this, he placed a picture of a giant, dirty sneaker taking up most of a living room and wrote, "At times, Robin walks all over Jim in a teasing, big brother manner." On the lower left and beneath a picture of three hats, Mr. McKee stated that Jim needed to just be himself instead of trying to imitate others by "wearing too many hats." Only one picture deals directly with the topic of the fighting; it shows a gang member from behind, in an aggressive stance and brandishing a knife. Next to this he wrote that because Jim cannot handle much teasing, Robin should know when to stop so that Jim does not feel "bad or picked on." This implies that Jim could not control himself and was not responsible for his behavior. The calm words are contrasted by the potential violence in the image.

In an effort to strengthen the parental subsystem and disentangle the child-parent alliances, I requested that Mr. and Mrs. McKee meet as a couple for a half hour before the family sessions. Despite repeated requests, it was rare that both parents would attend therapy simultaneously, and not once did the couple attend without any children. Usually, Mrs. McKee enjoyed this time as an opportunity for individual therapy.

At this point, I formulated a revised hypothesis for the family. I offered the family an interpretation of this hypothesis in the form of a drawing, described as follows.

Defining their system, the family homeostasis is represented as a balance scale. On one side of the scale, Mrs. McKee represents expression of emotionality. Her job is to express the family frustration, anger, and sadness with regular outbursts. Madonna, modeling after her mother, is also on this side of the balance scale. On the other side of the scale is Mr. McKee, who is delegated the job of calm, detached responsibility. He is not allowed to express emotion (which is Mrs. McKee's job). Robin, modeling after his father as "Mr. Cool," joins that side, balancing the scale.

Symbols were devised to represent metaphorically the two elements involved: water for overflowing emotion and rock for cool detachment. Using these symbols of the balance, water and rock, I drew the balance scale for the family.

I explained that so long as all members stick to the "rules" about how one is to behave, the family remains nicely balanced, until one considers

Jim. Jim's (scapegoat) role was interpreted to the family in the following manner. In order to maintain the balance, Jim has three choices: (1) he can either shift alliances, alternating between emotionality and detachment, quickly enough so that no one notices they are out of balance; (2) he must be altogether out of the picture (isolated from the family); or (3) he must remain at the center (deflecting attention onto himself through his behavior), while dealing with the job of "straddling the fence." Whichever choice is made, Jim has been placed in a difficult position. His actions can determine whether or not the family remains "balanced." I explained further that since this "job" was simply too difficult for a boy so young, they might consider an alternative.

If one large "water" (Mrs. McKee) and one large "rock" (Mr. McKee) shared one side of the scale, it might possibly balance against one small rock (Robin), one small water (Madonna), and a small combination of the two (Jim). The members could, if they desired, even borrow some emotionality or some responsibility from the others without upsetting the balance (allowing more freedom within their roles). This intervention graphically depicted the advantage of a strong parental subsystem.

When the idea was presented, Mrs. McKee's response was to look blank, followed by dawning understanding. In considering more responsibility for herself, she mentioned that she was looking for a job and would probably be working soon.

Although the boys appeared to be intrigued with the idea of changing the "balance," Mr. McKee's response was that the change would not work. He complained that Mrs. McKee would be unreliable in a responsible role and that she was unable to keep jobs for long. He added that he thought changes in the family structure were impractical and unworkable, again clarifying his resistance to change.

Since I was leaving my position at the clinic soon, plans were made toward terminating sessions with this family. Although continued family sessions would have been the treatment of choice, Jim stated that he did not want to come to family sessions. He did, however, wish to continue with his early-adolescent group therapy. In view of the family's inconsistent attendance and resistance to structural changes, Jim's continuance in group therapy was considered an acceptable alternative to "dropping out." Participating in the group would provide him with peer support and encourage appropriate individuation. It was recommended that Mrs. McKee allow herself to seek individual counseling to help deal with her depression. I encouraged the family to continue attending Alanon and Alateen.

Only Mrs. McKee and Jim attended the final session. I asked them to make a collage about saying goodbye. Mrs. McKee's pictures go past the edge of the page and overlap each other, reflecting her continuing poor sense of boundary. She framed the titles of three of her five pictures with musical notes. The largest image was of a rainbow over a castle, next to which she wrote, "At the end of a rainbow there is a pot of gold." When asked how the image related to the end of therapy, Mrs. McKee stated that she had made a collage about "goodbye" songs.

At the top right, her shoreline sunset was titled "Sunset, as the end of an era," also surrounded by musical notes. Above this, she wrote, "Dad, the sun rises and sets on you," signifying her co-dependent role and the centricity of the alcoholic. Beneath and overlapping the sunset is a picture of 10 ducks swimming away, and musically framed is, "Going home . . . we are going home; sad am I, glad am I, I am going home." I acknowledged that goodbyes are often accompanied by mixed or confused feelings. One of the ducks is swimming in a different direction from the others, much as I would go my separate way from the family.

At the bottom right is a picture of two men's hands shaking, one wearing the cufflink of an American flag and the other of a Canadian flag. Perhaps it illustrated the lack of shared effort and intent between the therapist and the family.

At the center top, and overlapping the rainbow and sunset, Mrs. McKee placed the picture of a young girl dressed in yellow sweatshirt and jeans, in a Superman pose, flying over a bay. Beneath the picture, she wrote, "Onward and upward, Jim; forward ho." This heroic image of Jim reminded me of his difficult role of maintaining the family homeostasis through his symptoms while being required to seek therapy for those same symptoms (placing him in a double bind).

Jim chose at first to perform one of his "tricks" by taking the alternative meaning from "goodbye" to "good buy." In a small picture of five salesmen smiling and excitedly displaying their products, Jim wrote "buy" in a bubble above their heads. The small image is centered on a sheet of black paper. This echoes Mrs. McKee's first drawing of the family in which the (five) members of the family may have been attempting to "sell" a misleading image of themselves. When I remarked on Jim's pun, he smiled and then asked to make a second collage.

In Figure 4.10, we see that Jim centered a cartoon on a blue sheet. It shows two trapeze performers with empty word "bubbles" above their heads (to be filled in by the client). As one performer is reaching out to keep the other from falling, the first one is also falling and looks perplexed. In the bubble of the first one, Jim wrote "AHHHHHHHHH! Goodbye, my good friend. AHHHHHHHHHHHHHHHHH HELP." Although the second performer states, "Just grab on . . . I will save you," the statement is followed by a large question mark. The performer has come loose from the swing in his effort to reach out. Jim's work reflects his sacrificial (scapegoat) position,

Figure 4.10. Jim's hopes and skepticism about therapy.

as well as his doubts about therapy's ability to make significant changes in the family. I was reminded of Jim's "Look at me" drawing produced months earlier.

The necessity for early termination with this family was particularly difficult and frustrating for me. The family's "consistently inconsistent" attendance and lack of motivation for change presented a formidable resistance. Despite the resistance, progress reports indicated that Jim's oppositional behavior had improved markedly over the period of therapy. During art therapy sessions, his rage and confusion were normalized and partially dissipated, while his self-esteem was raised through the accomplishment of his work.

In addition to Jim's personal progress, the parental subsystem had been strengthened with a firmer boundary, and Mrs. McKee was willing to work on improving her parenting skills. She was able to begin understanding how her husband's addiction and her own co-dependency affected her children's behavior. This new knowledge freed her to make choices toward change, whether or not Mr. McKee chose to recover from his addiction.

CONCLUSION

The significant value of art therapy with a family like this is that the concrete evidence presented in the form of art products is a powerful tool toward dealing with resistance. Regularly reviewing the art products serves to connect sessions and members who are absent intermittently, adding cohesion to the therapy. Communication patterns between family members can be defined and clarified. In addition, evidence presented in the art enables a family to view their relationships and dynamics from a new reference point. From this new reference point, it is hoped that steps toward healthier functioning are accomplished.

BIBLIOGRAPHY

Ackerman, R. J. (1983). *Children of Alcoholics. A Guidebook for Parents, Educators and Therapists* (2nd ed.). New York: Simon & Schuster.

Ackerman, R. J. (Ed.) (1986). *Growing in the Shadow: Children of Alcoholics*. Palm Beach, FL: Health Communications.

Albert-Puelo, N., & Osha, V. (1976–77). Art therapy as an alcohol treatment tool. *Alcohol Health and Research World, 1*(2), 28–31.

Anderson, C. M., & Stewart, S. (1983). *Mastering Resistance: A Practical Guide to Family Therapy*. New York: Guilford Press.

Barry, K. L., & Fleming, M. F. (1990). Family cohesion, expressiveness, and conflict in alcoholic families. *British Journal of Addiction, 85*(1), 81–87.

Beardslee, W. R., Son, L., & Vaillant, G. E. (1986). Exposure to parental alcoholism during childhood and outcome in adulthood: A prospective longitudinal study. *British Journal of Psychiatry, 149*, 584–591.

Bekhtel, E. E. (1986, summer). Psychological defense mechanisms in the clinical picture of alcoholism. *Soviet Neurology and Psychiatry*, 64–72.

Benson, C. S., & Heller, K. (1987). Factors in the current adjustment of young adult daughters of alcoholic and problem drinking fathers. *Journal of Abnormal Psychology, 96*(4), 305–312.

Black, C. (1981). *It Will Never Happen to Me. (Children of Alcoholics as Youngsters, Adolescents, Adults)*. Denver: M.A.C. Publications.

Black C. (1989). *It's Never Too Late to Have a Happy Childhood*. New York: Ballantine Books.

Boss, P. (1977, Feb.). A clarification of psychological father presence in families experiencing ambiguity of boundary. *Journal of Marriage and the Family*, 141–150.

Boss, P., & Greenberg, J. (1984). Family boundary ambiguity: A new variable in family stress theory. *Family Process, 23*, 535–546.

Callan, V. J., & Jackson, D. (1986). Children of alcoholic fathers and recovered alcoholic fathers: Personal and family functioning. *Journal of Studies of Alcohol, 47*(2), 180–182.

Deutsche, C. (1982). *Broken Bottles, Broken Dreams: Understanding and Helping the Children of Alcoholics*. New York: Teachers College Press.

Devine, D. K. (1970). A preliminary investigation of paintings by alcoholic men. *American Journal of Art Therapy, 9*(3), 115–129.

El-Guebaly, N., & Offord, D. R. (1977). The offspring of alcoholics: A critical review. *American Journal of Psychiatry, 134*(4), 357–365.

Ford, F. R. (1983). Rules: The invisible family. *Family Process, 22*(2), 135–145.

Forrest, G. (1975). The problems of dependency and the value of art therapy as a means of treating alcoholism. *Art Psychotherapy, 2*, 25–43.

Gromberg, E. (1989). On terms used and abused: The concept of codependency. *Drugs and Society, 3*(3–4), 113–132.

Hanson, G., & Liber, G. (1989). A moral for treatment of the adolescent child of an alcoholic. *Alcoholism Treatment Quarterly, 6*(2), 53–69.

Heilbrun, A. B., Jr. (1964). Parental model attributes, nurturant reinforcement, and consistency of behavior in adolescents. *Child Development, 35*, 151–167.

Hibbard S. (1989). Personality and object relational pathology in young adult children of alcoholics. *Psychotherapy, 26*(4), 504–509.

Hilton, M. E. (1987). Drinking patterns and drinking problems in 1984: Results from a general population survey. *Alcoholism: Clinical and Experimental Research, 11*(2), 167–175.

Jacob, T., Favorini, A., Meisel, S., & Anderson, C. (1978). The alcoholic's spouse, children and family interactions. *Journal of Studies on Alcohol, 39*(7), 1231–1251.

Knoblauch, D., & Bowers, N. D. (1989). A therapeutic conceptualization of adult children of alcoholics. *Journal of College Student Psychotherapy, 4*(1), 37–52.

Landgarten, H. (1981). *Clinical Art Therapy. A Comprehensive Guide*. New York: Brunner/ Mazel.

Landgarten, H. (1987). *Family Art Psychotherapy*. New York: Brunner/Mazel.

Leikin, C. (1986, Feb.). Identifying and treating the alcoholic client. *Social Casework*, 67–73.

Mann, M. (1981). *Marty Mann's New Primer on Alcoholism*. New York: Holt, Rinehart & Winston.

Miller, B., Downs, W. R., & Gondoli, D. M. (1989). Delinquency, childhood violence and the development of alcoholism in women. *Crime and Delinquency, 35*(1), 94–108.

McCabe, T. (1978). *Victims No More*. Center City, MN: Hazelden Educational Materials.

Molgaard, C. A., Chambers, C. M., Golbeck, A. C., Elder, J. P., et al. (1989). Maternal alcoholism and anorexia nervosa: A possible association? *International Journal of the Addictions, 24*(2), 167–173.

Moore, R. W. (1983). Art therapy with substance abusers: A review of the literature. *Arts in Psychotherapy, 10*, 260.

Nardi, P. M. (1981). Children of alcoholics: A role-theoretical perspective. *Journal of Social Psychology, 115*, 237–245.

Potter, P. S. (1989). Abuse in adult children of substance dependents: Effects and treatment. *Journal of Chemical Dependency Treatment, 3*(1), 99–129.

Phillips, A. M., Martin, D., & Martin, M. (1987). Counseling families with an alcoholic parent. *Family Therapy, 14*(1), 9–16.

Schafer, E. S. (1965). Children's reports of parental behavior: An inventory. *Child Development, 36*, 413–424.

Schlitt, R. (1986, Dec.). Childhood social support deficits of alcoholic women. *Social Casework*, 579–586.

Schuckit, M. A. (1985). Relationship between the course of primary alcoholism in men and family history. *Journal of Studies on Alcohol, 45*(4), 334–338.

Seixus, J. S., & Youcha, G. (1985). *Children of Alcoholism: A Survivor's Manual*. New York: Crown Publishers.

Stark, E. (1987). Forgotten victims: Children of alcoholics. *Psychology Today, 21*(1), 58–62.

The Twelve Steps for Adult Children. (1987). San Diego, CA: Recovery Publications.

Warner, R. H., & Rosett, H. L. (1975). The effects of drinking on offspring. *Journal of Studies on Alcohol, 36*(11), 1395–1420.

Webster, D., Harburg, E., Gleiberman, L., Schork, A., et al. (1989). Familial transmission of alcohol use. I. Parent and adult offspring alcohol use over 17 years—Tecumseh, Michigan. *Journal of Studies on Alcohol, 50*(1), 557–566.

Wegsheider, S. (1976). *No One Escapes from a Chemically Dependent Family*. Crystal, MN: Nurturing Networks.

Wegsheider, S. (1979). Children of alcoholics caught in family trap. *Focus on Alcohol and Drug Issues, 2*, 8.

West, M. O., & Prinz, R. J. (1987). Parental alcoholism and childhood psychopathology. *Psychological Bulletin, 102*(2), 204–218.

Wilmuth, M., & Boedy, D. L. (1979). The verbal diagnostic and art therapy combined: An extended evaluation procedure with family groups. *Art Psychotherapy, 6*, 11–18.

Wilson, C., & Orford, J. (1978). Children of alcoholics (Report of a preliminary study and comments on the literature). *Journal of Studies on Alcohol, 39*(1), 121–142.

Woititz, J. (1986). Common characteristics of adult children from alcoholic families. In R. J. Ackerman (Ed.), *Growing in the Shadow*. Palm Beach, FL: Health Communications.

Wolin, S. J., & Bennett, L. A. (1984). Family rituals. *Family Process, 23*, 401–420.

−5−

Family Art Therapy
and Sexual Abuse

Denise Cross

The 12-week introductory group program for sexually abused children described in this chapter was designed for a small community mental health facility that offered family therapy, but wished to supplement it with group experience.* Group treatment for victims of molestation has been documented repeatedly as an important component in the healing process, and the design here was a modified multifamily group milieu with females and their nonoffending mothers. Recognizing the generational nature of molestation (James & Nasjleti, 1983; Russell, 1986), the co-leaders felt that it was important to include the mothers in the hope of interrupting the cycle.

The art therapy modality was used for several reasons. Children's love of fantasy and play makes art an ideal medium for addressing their conflicts in a manner that elicits the highest level of competence and comfort. It also provides structure and distance to emotions that may seem overwhelming, frightening, or confusing by allowing their expression via metaphor. It is through the understanding and awareness of the metaphor's message that the healing process may take place.

When incest begins at a preverbal stage, art provides a way of communicating without verbal skills. A natural medium for children, art also is not usually subject to years of rigid defense building, as is verbal expression (Goodwin, 1982); thus, this offers equal advantage—and disadvantage—to all group participants, no matter the age. There is an immediate sense of tangible creation, as well. And creativity, when supported naturally, enhances self-esteem, self-worth, and, most important, self-trust (Naitove, 1982; Carozza & Heirsteiner, 1983; Stember, 1980).

Before one can fully comprehend treatment concerns, it is important to

---

*Thanks to Ginger Kershner, ATR, MFCC, for her help in creating and facilitating this project.

understand the family dynamics and the social context that characteristically support sexual abuse. Many authors (Burgess, Groth, Holmstrom, & Sgroi, 1978; Rush, 1980; Sgroi, 1982; James & Nasjleti, 1983; Russell, 1986) agree that incest and molestation seem to be related to issues of power and dominance rather than being strictly sexual aberrations. Russell especially feels it is a result of biases in a male-dominated society that sees women and children as possessions with little status.

There are several descriptions that apply to family systems that perpetuate incest and victimization. Frequently, the father is threatened by sexual relations with an adult female and uses his position of power over his child to feel potent. In other cases, the male is misogynous or tyrannical, mistreating and subjugating all family members he deems "weaker." Some authors reported that the males often had been molested themselves as children, creating severe confusion about gender identity and boundaries (Groth, 1982; Bolton, 1989). Often, the mothers are unable or unwilling to protect the children, sacrificing them to maintain the security of a relationship with their mate.

What is most often seen within these family systems is an inappropriate expression of feelings, an erosion of self-trust, and a lack of appropriate acceptance of responsibility. That the cultural institutions support these same dynamics (i.e., laws that do not protect victims and often revictimize; lack of accountability for offenders within the legal system; pervasive messages by institutions and in the literature that the victim is at fault) enhances one's awareness of the magnitude of the cultural and historical bias (Russell, 1986). This skewing within the family is only a reflection of a general skewing in the greater society.

Studies by Janoff-Bulman and Frieze (1983) suggest that the psychological damage of abuse comes from the shattering of some basic assumptions that children have about themselves and their world—including a belief in personal invulnerability, a perception of the world as meaningful and comprehensible, and a positive view of themselves. I have often heard survivors state that self-doubt is the most eroding result of abuse. In families that deny the occurrence of abuse, the repercussions are severe. The victims fear that they will not be believed by others and eventually begin to doubt that the molestations occurred at all.

This is an insidious process, as it is connected to external sensory input (pain, pressure, touch) and internal sensory input (feelings of fear, anger, love, survival) in which the child eventually does not believe. Without this accurate verification, the child tries to make some sense from this conflict between what he or she knows at an intuitive level and what the "authorities" dictate. Because, in most cases, adults are considered the authority by virtue of their knowledge and power, the abused child usually dismisses his or her own information in an attempt at resolution (Bass & Davis, 1988).

To maintain this version of conflict resolution, however, the child must continue to dismiss his or her own internal and external information; this is most often accomplished through the mental construct of a defense mechanism that alters input. In essence, the mechanism for accurately evaluating information has been tampered with. There is a rigidity of response to stimulus that is the mask for a deep confusion as to what is true. This is certainly not a rich environment for the processing of information, especially any that conflicts with the rigid mind-set. How can such children, growing into adulthood, really trust what they see in themselves or the world? How can they claim the full spectrum of human responses when they and society, deny their internal truth?

I feel that it is the task of the therapist to be an accurate mirror for those inner and outer sensations of the survivor, thereby acknowledging the truth of the client's experience and fostering a greater trust in his or her own assessments. This is the first task of human development as identified by Erikson (1950), but it is one that is rarely achieved in an incestuous relationship.

Molestation by trusted friends, extended-family members, and strangers can have this same impact if the child is revictimized by attitudes that suppress accurate expression (Russell, 1986; Driver & Droisen, 1989). Without support for and encouragement of expression, the feelings are subject to defenses that suppress internal conflict. This is an imperfect solution. The conflict is only submerged rather than resolved and is likely to surface as maladaptive behavior, such as an addiction or behavioral problems (Finklehor, 1979; James & Nasjleti, 1983; Russell, 1986). Ideally, the maladaptive behaviors disappear when the inner conflicts finally surface and are explored truthfully.

OVERVIEW OF GROUP MODEL

The topics presented for discussion in the 12-week model attempt to address the most salient issues common to molestation cases (Sgroi, 1983; Russell, 1986; Bass & Davis, 1988). Our efforts were directed toward a group experience that would encourage the expression of each client's conflicts, identify feelings, build self-trust and self-respect, and increase a sense of power through assertion. (Russell [1986] suggests that assertive behavior on the part of victims may discourage some potential abusers.) As stated earlier, this group was seen as an adjunct to family therapy. The participants (described below) changed frequently during the 12 weeks, which was not unusual in the population served by this clinic—a low socioeconomic status community with few resources and multiple levels of stressors. Weekly attendance was encouraged, but an open-door policy was considered best for parents who already seemed overwhelmed with financial, social, and psychological pressures. The objectives and material presentation for each week's session were followed by an interpretation of some of the artwork and a brief discussion of the participants' general responses.

The format of most sessions was fairly routine. A story, skit, or other presentation related to the week's topic started the session, followed by a short discussion period to ensure the participants' understanding of the material. An art directive was given to stimulate an emotional response to the information. Clients were provided with the opportunity to discuss their artwork and listen to other members.

At first, mothers were encouraged to help their children to maintain appropriate behavior and to assist them as needed in art projects. The goal was to increase parenting skills through modeling and guidance, educate parents on molestation issues, and increase child-parent interaction. We planned to slowly integrate parents into participating in art projects during later sessions.

DESCRIPTION OF THE GROUP MEMBERS

Renée, age five, attended with her mother. Presenting behaviors included refusal to obey her parents, fights with other children, destruction of property, and regressive behavior. Her sexual abuse history was reported as molestation by a seven-year-old neighbor who used metal cars for vaginal penetration.

Mary, age five, attended with her maternal grandmother. Behaviors include aggression toward her sister, excessive masturbation, oppositional behavior, and general separation anxiety. Abuse was reported as sexual exploration by her mother's boyfriend. Mary was removed from her mother's care after her mother's failed suicide attempt. The mother had tried to fill the entire house with gas while the children were inside.

Daphne, eight years old, attended with her aunt. She came to the clinic because of her lying and stealing, fighting with peers, excessive masturbation, and suicidal ideation. Her sexual abuse history indicated that she had been molested repeatedly by a great-uncle, which included mutual masturbation. Her parents are heavy drug abusers and her father left her with his brother and sister-in-law to raise after the disclosure of the molestation. The uncle and aunt want to adopt Daphne.

Debbie, three years old, attended sessions with her mother. Her behavior was reported as being oppositional and marked by sexual play with dolls, hitting of friends, sleep disturbances, and excessive masturbation. Her abuse history was reported as cunnilingus by her father for the past year.

Nancy was eight years old and came to group with her mother. Her behavior was reported as disruptive in the classroom, hyperactive, and characterized by sexualized actions and excessive masturbation. Her sexual abuse history indicates that she had been abused by her stepbrother for the past few years, including mutual fondling, kissing, and insertion of objects into her vagina.

Kimberly, age seven, attended sessions with her mother. Her presenting problem behaviors included suicidal ideation, nightmares, and oppositional actions. It was reported that her father played "mouth" games and bit her during visitations. A custody battle had been in progress since the abuse was disclosed.

DISCUSSION OF SESSIONS

Session 1 was a parents-only introductory session. The purpose was to discuss sexual abuse issues, explain the necessity for group experience for this population, and have the parents meet one another. We presented the preventative aspect of the program that was designed to discourage revictimization. What became clear in the question-and-answer period at this session was the lack of awareness of how molestation or any traumatic experience was affecting the children's behavior. This was really a new concept for these parents and, in retrospect, we realized that more time should have been devoted to educating these mothers and guardians. Initial contact with these women seemed successful, but the material was overwhelming, even in its tailored form.

Session 2 included the children and their parent/guardians. The topic was body image. The purpose of the art project was to introduce the concept of boundaries and the integrity of the body, as well as to stimulate thoughts of positive self-care and body image. Each child was given a reproduction of an outlined human figure to color. The images would then be placed on the outside of individual folders, which would be the receptacles for future artwork produced in the group. The external image on the folder was viewed as a symbolic representation of the child's self. Several other outlined pictures showing self-care (children brushing teeth, washing, safely crossing streets, etc.) were also provided for coloring and discussion. The object of these pictures was to stimulate thoughts of positive self-care and to explore body image.

To maintain optimum structure, thereby minimizing the level of initial anxiety, we placed the children and parents around a large table, which allowed each individual ample personal space. Art supplies were introduced

Figure 5.1. Renee shows self-aggression.

only when the art project directive was given. During the first few sessions, art supplies were handed to each child until a tolerance for sharing was established. Gradually, after the cohesiveness and norms of the group solidified, the external structure was slowly removed and group projects were encouraged.

The artwork of all three girls attending the first two sessions displayed a characteristic anxiety regarding their bodies. The degree of control over this anxiety varied greatly with each child. Renée's artwork, which demonstrated the least amount of control, and her group behavior, which ventilated her anxiety, will be discussed in more detail.

Renée's treatment of her outlined figure (Figure 5.1) could be seen as a display of self-aggression. She applied orange and blue with heavy, pressured lines. The concentration of color below the neck might indicate her preoccupation with the body and the separation she feels between her head and violated body. When cutting out her figure, she seemed particularly vicious. Part of the right hand was removed and the right foot was deliberately cut off (this was eventually glued to the folder with the help of her mother). There is a deep gash in the genital area that extends to the pelvic area.

After completing the self-care pictures, Renée scribbled over the ''child in bed'' and the ''bath'' pictures (Figure 5.2). She applied pressure and attempted to obliterate the faces. It had been reported that Renée was molested by a young male neighbor, but her behavior and pictures seemed to indicate additional problems associated with her home. It was later learned

Figure 5.2. Hidden problems at home?

that there was an uncle living in the house, but this had not been mentioned by the parents in family therapy. Renée's behavior during the session became increasingly oppositional. She threw pen caps across the table and sat on the table rather than in the chair. Her mother did little to correct these behaviors.

Excessive permissiveness and lack of limit-setting were major issues in family treatment for Renée. She was molested again during the first week after this session. Her family had again failed to supervise and protect her adequately. Her pictures seem to reflect a creature unworthy of protection. Renée did not return to group, but remained in family treatment.

In the third week, we attempted to encourage a rudimentary awareness of four specific feeling states, which would then be associated with resultant behavior. Feelings would be explored as transitory and/or conflictual experiences. They would be presented as a partial expression rather than the totality of the child's self. Four pie plates with handles were given to each child, and the children were instructed to make a mask for each of four emotions— mad, sad, happy, and scared.

Most of the girls were able to do this task with relative ease. In general, their masks for each feeling had an appropriate corresponding expression. Two interesting observations were made with regard to Mary and her grandmother and to Debbie. Debbie completed all the masks without her mother's help. While three of the masks had recognizable facial features, the mask marked "scared" seemed to display considerable turmoil (Figure 5.3). She dotted the "face" with many circles and heavy pen gashes. This is often indicative of anxiety and conflict. Her other masks did not display this level of disturbance.

Mary's mask production proceeded slowly, with much interference and criticism from her grandmother. This grandmother revealed that she had been molested as a child, but denied lingering effects from the experience. She strongly believed that forgetting the incident was better for her granddaughter and for herself. As the criticism and interference continued, the grandmother abruptly took three of the masks and completed them herself. This seemed to indicate an unconscious desire to express her own unresolved feelings and we attempted to facilitate her needs. Despite these efforts, within the next few weeks, this woman would terminate treatment and would relinquish guardianship of Mary and return her to a neglectful mother.

Session 4 presented a discussion of the difference between ''surprises'' and ''secrets.'' The objective was to place the responsibility for molestation on the perpetrator rather than on the child. A squiggle technique was used to distance the children from actual experiences. They were instructed to color their squiggles with colors that represented secrets and surprises respectively. Surprises were defined as a secret that could eventually be expressed. Secrets were seen as experiences or feelings the child was asked to keep hidden. It was clearly communicated in the presentation period that secrets regarding molestation were detrimental. An emphasis was also placed on whom the children could confide in when they wanted to divulge a secret.

A comparison of the children's two drawings showed that all the ''secret'' pictures received a greater investment of energy, time, and emotion. Interestingly, all the children chose black and red as the colors to represent the secrets. There was a general attempt to control the anxiety stimulated during the creation of the pictures by encapsulating the images. Most of the children

Figure 5.3.   Debbie's emotion masks.

do not tell no one
that I stuck my
tongue out?

Figure 5.4. Daphne's "secret" drawing.

applied the colors in heavy, pressured strokes, sometimes allowing colors to bleed through the page.

Daphne produced the most striking of the secret drawings (Figure 5.4). She outlined a large mouth that resembled a vaginal orifice. There was heavy shading along the top of the image and a yellow, unidentified structure that dipped into its center. The "mouth" seemed to be open and menacing with what looks like a dark drool oozing from the interior. The zigzag pattern emanating outward from the interior appeared sharp, jagged, and threatening.

The suggestion of oral/vaginal sexuality this picture evokes does not coincide with the abuse reported by this child, but suggests more extensive sexual abuse than originally believed. The message written on the side that warns about telling hints at Daphne's struggle in disclosing this secret. In truth, her disclosure resulted in her removal from her neglectful household. The disruption of the family structure is a reality for these children that needs addressing. This is often what the perpetrator threatens, and what the nonoffending parent wants to avoid. The children should receive clear messages that they are not responsible for, nor must they endure, a dysfunctional family's behavior.

Session 5 was a parents-only group meeting. The object was to discuss the mothers' or guardians' experiences since the beginning of the 12 weeks. We felt flexible in our approach to this meeting. Art directives could be introduced that focused on feelings of the parents toward their children, on how they were dealing with the molestation, or on more discussion regarding their children's behavior. Since the session was attended by only one parent, it became obvious that its scheduling was premature. A decision was made to schedule these ''parent'' sessions only when group cohesion had formed.

The topic for session 6 was ''comfortable'' and ''uncomfortable'' touches. The objective was to educate and identify areas of the body that are considered ''private.'' Again, the issues of boundaries and individual integrity were presented. The art directive asked the children to look at collage material and pick out three picture that displayed comfortable and uncomfortable touches.

Nancy and her mother joined the group as new participants. The other members of the group were asked to review the material from previous weeks to help orient Nancy and to assess the retention of information. The regular group members had little difficulty in picking out appropriate pictures for each subject, but Nancy seemed to be confused when attempting to differentiate the two types of touches. This conflict became evident in her collage, where she could not decide whether one of her pictures was comfortable or uncomfortable.

This confusion seemed to center around a picture of a man at a doctor's office; he had wires and electrodes connected to a machine (Figure 5.5). Nancy repeatedly crossed out the words ''good'' and ''bad'' under this picture. Her anxiety was displayed in an inability to remain seated during much of the session. The conflict evoked by this picture was not realized until several days later when Nancy disclosed to her mother that her brother and sister had forced her to play ''doctor'' with them and had used toy medical implements for insertion.

The seventh-week session attempted to focus on the issue of nightmares. The objective was to teach assertion skills to reduce or eliminate nightmare

Figure 5.5.   An ''uncomfortable touch'' picture evokes Nancy's anxiety.

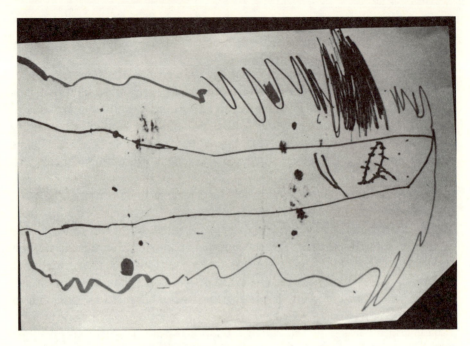

Figure 5.6. Debbie's "clown."

occurrences. This would build self-trust, self-assurance, and the use of individual power and strength. The children were asked to draw a picture of their nightmare, thereby distancing and reducing it to manageable size. Then they were encouraged to practice assertive skills in demanding that the image leave them alone. They were also allowed to tear or destroy the image in whatever way they wished.

Debbie refused to draw a nightmare, but instead made a shape she titled "elephant." On the other side of the sheet of paper, she drew what she called "clown." The shape, with a mouth ringed with sharp, jagged teeth,

Figure 5.7. Mary's monster.

resembled a penis (Figure 5.6). The anxiety this picture evoked was evident in the heavy, scribbled red line she drew in the upper corner. She took a red marker and jabbed the ''clown'' repeatedly. The strokes were purposeful, delivered with great force and energy. She then delivered repeated pen slashes to the ''elephant'' in the same angry manner. After making the pen marks, Debbie drew a circle around the picture, probably in an attempt to contain the emotional outburst. She refused to join the other group members in the verbal assertive-skill exercise.

Mary became very absorbed in this project, drawing monsters on both sides of her paper (Figures 5.7 and 5.8). She added a multitude of pen jabs and made circles around the images, producing a chaotic, swirling effect. Mary's initial attempts at assertion were timid, but with encouragement they changed into loud bellows. Her delight at this new-found strength was evident in her erect posture, her impish grin, and her repeated requests to continue the bellowing. Mary was an excellent role model for Nancy, who was eventually able to yell at her own nightmare picture to ''leave her alone.''

The ''damaged goods'' syndrome, the belief that one is permanently damaged by the abuse, was the topic for session 8. We began by reading a story about a girl who had lost something very precious, a red ribbon. Her fear was that she would not be accepted without the ribbon. The concepts of loss and transformation were the thrust of this exercise. Each child was asked to draw a picture that told about a time when she felt like the girl in the story or about an unpleasant experience. After this, a template would be used to pick out the one part of the picture she liked. This piece would be added to a group decoration of a butterfly.

Figure 5.8.   Additional monsters by Mary.

Before the project began, group members were introduced to Kimberly and her mother. Time was spent on introductions and discussion of the departure of Mary and her grandmother, who had terminated treatment. The children were provided with smaller sheets of paper to facilitate a rapid completion and contain anxiety. Broken blue circles on the color plates indicate areas cut from original pictures.

All of the children had some difficulty with this assignment. The subject was a direct reference to their molestation and the artwork reflected the anxiety associated with the experience.

Daphne's artwork seemed regressive and small compared with her previous productions (Figure 5.9). Her first attempt was a small, helpless figure without hands or feet, seen at the top of the page. She then crossed this out and drew on the other side of the paper. This time she produced a purple figure whose feet moved away from the threat. She gave it red paddlelike hands, which may reflect anger, but the arms remained in an open vulnerable position. She identified the fragmented figure in brown as an "attacker." It is obvious how much anxiety is associated with the brown figure, which is barely recognizable as a human form.

During the first part of this project, there was a palpable intensity in the group. Mothers or guardians worked quietly with their children to assist in using the round template. There was no interference with what the child eventually chose as the part to cut out. After this, we introduced the concept of transformation, that experiences do not have to remain unchanged. The tables were cleared and placed together, additional art materials were introduced, and parents were encouraged to participate.

The mothers became very excited and enthusiastic. Daphne's aunt was the only adult who participated minimally. There was a great deal of playfulness as mothers and daughters worked together in a group effort to decorate the butterfly. The mothers applied many rainbows and flowers to the dull butterfly (Figure 5.10). Although this can be interpreted as their attempts to gloss over the difficult feelings stirred by the first pictures, the atmosphere in the group had definitely shifted. Mothers and children interacted with each other and with other families. There was a sense of sharing and cooperation not seen before. The children and parents left the room at the end of group excited and involved.

The ninth week began with the news that Daphne would no longer be participating in the group, but instead she would continue individual treatment, as her aunt and uncle refused to attend family sessions. We had been concerned that there was little emotional investment in Daphne by the aunt and uncle. The aunt's minimal interaction in the last group session seemed to be a reflection of the home situation. Daphne was given the necessities

Figure 5.9. The ''damaged goods'' syndrome.

Figure 5.10. Mothers and daughters work together.

for existence and a stable environment, but a loving bond with her guardians remained elusive.

The topic for the ninth week was the issue of guilt. The object was to be able to recognize that sexual abuse is often associated with a child's need for love, affection, and approval. Children usually believe that if they have these natural desires, then they also must have wanted the abuse that goes along with them. Previously positive emotions (love, acceptance, etc.) are now linked with the incest experience. A conditioned response is formed; whenever the children want love or feel loving, they begin to reexperience the guilt and/or shame of the abuse. A book was read to the group. Its theme was the concept that often there are experiences that one enjoys, and yet this is separate from what one may be asked to do for that enjoyment. We hoped that this would help the children to recognize all the feelings associated with the abuse (rage, depression, pain, excitement, etc.) in a nonjudgmental way.

Plasticene was offered to the group members with which to make sculptures. Mothers were encouraged to help as their children directed. The parents were to participate in the second half of this project, another joint venture with their children. Before this could happen, Kimberly's art production took the focus of the rest of the session. Her process will be discussed in greater detail.

Kimberly worked with her mother and produced a family sculpture consisting of a father and mother (who looked remarkably alike) and a child. When she finally designated one of the adult figures as the ''mother,'' Kim insisted that a mouth be omitted. Omissions are often a way to indicate that the anatomical part is inadequate or is incapable of functioning. After completion of the three figures, Kim's mother encouraged her child with probing questions to disclose the molestation incident (the mother's inability to discuss the incident underscored the missing mouth on the figurine).

Using the plasticene character, Kim told the group that when she was a baby, her father did not hurt her, but when she was a small child, he had pinched her buttocks during a weekend visitation. After relating this, she grabbed the child figure from the arms of the father and began to tear it to pieces. Her mother became visibly shaken and attempted to collect the pieces and put them together. Kim repeatedly grabbed the figure from her mother to mash it. The co-leaders intervened and asked Kim about her feelings regarding the molestation. It was difficult for her to verbalize at first. She was able to comment on what had happened by using the figures. Finally, she talked about how she had wanted her father to behave. She then decided to change her sculpture.

Kim was allowed control over the project and directed each group member to make some part of the new sculpture. She first wanted the child figure to

Figure 5.11.   Kim remodels a family sculpture.

be made into a baby. She had her mother make the baby from the torn pieces of the plasticene child. Other members were asked to make a cradle, blanket, pillows, dolls, and food. Kim delegated work to each member deftly, indicating that she wanted the baby to be safe.

We encouraged Kim to change the sculpture to fit her needs. She placed the father by the cradle of the baby. She added a mouth to the mother figure and also placed her next to the cradle. She had the mother figure vigilantly watching the father figure (Figure 5.11).

Kim was able to address many issues in the production of her sculpture: her displaced anger at herself (tearing the child figure); anger regarding her mother's inability to speak out (missing mouth); the molestation by her father. Much was accomplished in the remodeling of the sculpture: her continued love for and need of her father's presence (placing him by the cradle); her wish to have her mother's protection from further harm (the mother figure given a mouth and watching the dad); her need to be cared for and nurtured, especially by her mother (making the child into a baby); her desire to have the group support her (having all members participate in the resculpting). It was particularly difficult to end this session after the expression of such intense emotions. Closure was accomplished by comments on this process.

Temper tantrums would be the topic for the 10th week. The objective was to encourage recognition of the connection between the anger and the resultant acting-out behavior. The art project would focus on the children's producing a sculpture of how they look when they have angry feelings. The mothers would be asked to make a "safe" place for the angry child. This was discussed in terms of parenting skills, so the children could not hurt themselves or others.

We learned in this session that it was premature to ask these parents to produce a safe environment for their children having tantrums. It would have been wiser to ask them to make a picture about how they felt when their children were acting out. These parents had their own inner child with tantrums and no safe place for ventilation. This was particularly evident in the artwork produced by Nancy and her mother.

Upon entering the group, Nancy's mother had revealed that their family session had been particularly intense. Nancy had confronted her mother on lack of protection. She was visibly agitated and had a great deal of difficulty remaining in her seat. She frequently made derogatory comments about her mother, who passively accepted them with few attempts at control.

Nancy produced a round figure with tentacle-like legs, smiling face, and bulging eyes. She made a long, green sausage shape and covered the end with white plasticene. She took this phallic symbol to her mouth, pretending to lick it. This green shape was then jammed into the tentacle figure. She finally removed the green shape and completely destroyed the tentacled figure.

Her mother produced the "safe" place (Figure 5.12). It was a stark, empty square with a small window high in the upper corner. There was nothing else in the room but a door. It strongly resembled a prison cell. It was evident that this was the punishment room for her daughter's behavior—

Figure 5.12.   A mother's "safe" place.

a passive-aggressive response that characterized the mother-daughter relationship. When Nancy was asked if she wanted anything in the room, she mentioned a lion, ice cream, rain, and a doll. Her mother drew them all, but the room remained sterile and unfriendly.

This mother was very hostile about her daughter's disclosure. Her favorite child, her son, had been removed from the home because of the report. She constantly commented on her conflicting feelings regarding his revealed abusive behavior. Comforting or supporting her daughter was almost impossible when she continued to be assailed by new reports of criminal behavior by her beloved male child. Nancy gave a group member's name to each of the objects in her "safe" place. She seemed to recognize that the group could provide her with the support and understanding that her mother could not give.

The 11th session was devoted to the production of a gameboard and game pieces that would be used the following week. The object of the game was to present a review of all the previous weeks' topics. The game pieces would be made by the children from plasticene. The board was constructed with the help of the parents. The parents and children would first apply squares of colored paper linearly. On either side of the line of colored squares would be pictures grouped according to previous weeks' topics.

The game itself was simple. A color wheel spinner was used and the child's game piece would advance to the appropriate color. The child would be asked a "what if" question that corresponded to the picture group. For example, if she landed by the pictures from the week on feelings, she might be asked, "If you were angry with a friend, what would you say/do?" Or if she landed on the square close to touching, the question might be, "What if someone touched you and it made you feel uncomfortable?" The questions could be general at first and more specific as the children's anxiety decreased. In this game, the answers are used for further learning, elaborating, and strengthening of assertive skills. There is a starting line and a finish line; the children advance when the answer is accepted by the group as correct.

The children worked with one of us to make their game pieces. Kim and Nancy's choice was "Sunshine Care Bear." They picked a lovable, huggable, happy, fantasy creature that is connected to an extended supportive family. Debbie made an owl as her game piece. If we interpret this from the perspective of group consciousness, both Kim and Nancy seem to trust and accept the group as indicated by what they were willing to reveal in art productions. Like the owl, Debbie was aloof, observing, and watchful, not yet ready to join the others. Although Debbie enjoyed attending group sessions, she still rarely participated verbally, continuing to whisper to her mother, who would then address the group.

While the children worked on their game pieces, the mothers were engaged in the construction of the game board. (The mothers and children had picked out the pictures earlier in the session.) As the mothers worked, they began to discuss their common problems with their individual children. A camaraderie began to emerge as the similarities in experience and expression became evident. Strategies were discussed for handling problematic behavior. They avidly compared and contrasted their interactions with school systems, courts, support systems, relatives, and so on, trading both positive and negative experiences. These parents seemed starved for an opportunity to discuss their problems with other women who had had similar experiences. It was difficult to have them end the session.

Their discussion continued in front of the building after we had departed. We understood that these women needed a place in which to express their feelings, and find strength and support. That they were willing to risk this intimate interaction was their gift to each other and to their daughters. They were offered a parents-only group in two weeks. All agreed to attend.

Session 12 was devoted to playing the game. All three parents and the children attended. Kim and Nancy were eager to play, but Debbie became restless, refusing to answer any questions. Nancy remained relatively contained during the entire session, despite the difficulty of reviewing stimulating material from previous weeks.

The significance of this session will be discussed in terms of noticeable changes in each participant's behavior since entering the group. Kim began by discussing what she had learned about her body. Her assertive skills seemed strong and were a model for Nancy, who followed. This time, Nancy was quite able to identify comfortable and uncomfortable touches. She was also able strongly to voice objections, an obvious difference from the original session on touching. Debbie was able to avoid doing this exercise by provoking an argument with her mother.

When "secrets" were the topic, Kim revealed that her father had tried to persuade her to lie about his unmonitored visits. She had disclosed this fact to the babysitter although the father had threatened that if she told, she would never see him again. Significantly, Kim did not first reveal this fact to her mother. Her mother's response to the news was characteristically vitriolic toward the father. Kim's picture was of a man driving a boy in a car. Kim indicated that this showed a child who had difficulty talking to her parent (Figure 5.13, lower corner). The child looks sad, eyes cast down as if in shame; the male figure seems distant and angry. The child in this picture seems to epitomize Kim's dilemma—caught between warring parents, and believing herself shameful and responsible for their distress. The driver could symbolize either parent, for both are angry and withdrawn, holding Kim responsible for their problems.

In the same "secret" section, Nancy also chose an interesting picture,

Figure 5.13. Nancy's secret.

one with an older woman, a young boy, and a teenage girl (Figure 5.13, center). The face of the woman looks startled and pained as the small child in the middle puts a finger to his lips, requesting silence. This typifies Nancy's predicament as her mother continued to respond with horror and disbelief as the disclosures of abuse unfolded. The male child wanting silence could represent Nancy's brother, who is now separated from the family and faces criminal abuse charges. The boy seems concerned and somewhat fearful. The older girl in the picture looks resolute and determined. This older girl seems to represent Nancy's determination to continue the disclosures despite her mother's and brother's reactions. Most significant was the fact that, despite her mother's shocked response, Nancy now listed her as the first person to whom she would disclose negative secrets. In previous sessions, she had named everyone except her mother.

The pictures chosen to represent touching had sexually explicit themes for both Kim and Nancy. Nancy, whose sexual abuse was the most extensive, picked an extremely graphic representation of couples engaged in touching. Kim, whose reported sexual abuse was less extensive, picked a couple sleeping together. The picture is sexual in nature but tender in its treatment as compared with Nancy's choice. This is consistent with the reports of Nancy's molestation being more physically abusive than Kim's.

Debbie chose a picture of a child and a toy gas pump. The pump has a definite phallic presentation and the child at play may represent how Debbie was introduced to the abuse. While the other children practiced assertion skills, Debbie took two pieces from her owl game piece and covered the eyes of the boy playing with the gas pump. She finally removed them at the end of the exercise. This "blinding" while the child is at play may again reflect her lack of seeing or her ignorance of the abuse that was introduced to her as a "game." This theme is seen repeatedly in Debbie's pictures; the wish to deny the exploitation of the experience because of its many reinforcing qualities.

The session drew to an end with the awarding of certificates for the participants who had completed this first series. The parents-only group would meet the next week. Multifamily group sessions would continue, leading to greater intensity and expansion of issues in weeks ahead. Entry into this group would remain open, as agreed to by all members, to appropriately screened families. Old material would be reviewed and new material would be addressed as the group continued to solidify.

DISCUSSION OF GROUP'S EXPERIENCE

It is always difficult to evaluate so personal an experience as therapy. The effects on the individuals are often so subtle that an accurate measuring device remains elusive. The children and parents will be discussed as to changes in behaviors and expression that were observable. This will be our means of determining the effectiveness of treatment.

We had wanted to create an atmosphere of acceptance and safety for both parent and child. We felt that this would offer a fertile ground for exploring individual and collective potential. The use of a multifamily group allowed participants to observe other families in similar struggles. As we guided the families in self-exploration, the members supported each other through empathic consideration. We hoped that the result would be growth away from rigid, dysfunctional patterns of interaction as new behaviors were tried.

Renée left the group after the first session. She continued in family treatment, but with her father attending. It was learned that her mother suffered from an inoperable brain tumor and the focus of family treatment addressed this immediate issue. Her oppositional behavior greatly decreased as her father became skilled at limit-setting and as the issues around her mother's illness were discussed.

Mary and her grandmother left the sessions by the seventh week. She, like the other children, had an initial exacerbation of problematic behavior during treatment. Parental tolerance for this frequently observed response to psychotherapy requires a strong emotional bond. Mary's grandmother chose to send her to her mother. Similarly, Renée's mother chose withdrawal and Daphne's aunt chose separation. It is interesting that the three remaining participants (those able to tolerate continuing) were biological mothers and daughters.

All the remaining children also had an initial exacerbation of their problematic presenting behaviors. From a family-systems viewpoint, this might be seen as the last effort at homeostasis before shifting patterns emerge. As Nancy found strength in her assertive skills in group, her verbal attacks on her mother increased. Along with this was the development of her mother's alliance with other women in the group, who provided her with understanding and support concerning her divided loyalties to her daughter and son. She was able to attempt strategies for containing Nancy's behavior and to remain open to further disclosures. Three weeks after the last group session, Nancy was able to confront her mother on the issue of lack of protection. After this, her aggressive behavior and sexual acting out diminished considerably.

Kimberly presented as a quiet, compliant child. By the end of the first few sessions, her mother reported an increase in aggressive and angry outbursts. With increased encouragement, she was able to discuss openly her issues regarding her mother's boyfriends, her fears about remolestation, her feelings about her relationship with her father, and so on. By the 12th session, her suicidal ideation had been eliminated and her nightmares had decreased. Kim became one of the most articulate of the children and was a role model for the others in assertive skills. Her mother seemed to become less controlling of her as the angry feelings were openly discussed.

Debbie's and her mother's behavioral changes are most interesting, as Debbie was the youngest and least verbal and the family was the only one to attend all sessions. This child's original presentation was as suspicious and depressed. Her mother seemed overwhelmed and indecisive. With her mother, Debbie formed a closed symbiotic relationship marked by passive-aggressive behaviors. As with the other children, by the middle of the 12-week course, Debbie was overtly expressing anger through outbursts. This was challenged by her mother's increased strength as a disciplinarian, a position supported by the group women and by education in effective parenting techniques. By the 12th week, Debbie's behavior had changed radically.

Not only were most of her presenting problems resolving, but she looked happy and appeared less suspicious. Debbie's mother was calmer, was more direct in expressing anger, and showed greater self-assurance in dealing with her daughter. Debbie was able to separate from her mother, which previously had been impossible, to play with the other group children alone, and to attend preschool.

Daphne, the last of the children to be discussed, ended group treatment prematurely, but continued to work on these issues with her family therapist. Her artwork was particularly interesting in that initially it showed strong defenses in the use of bold colors and lines. In her last session, her drawings displayed vulnerability and weakness in small, monochromatic, poorly constructed figures. She revealed that the group was important because she knew that others had experienced molestation. Her feelings had been validated by the other children; she no longer felt stigmatized and alone. Daphne produced a book about what she had learned from the group. Its focus was the importance of her body. After sharing this book with her therapist, there was a corresponding decrease in her acting-out behavior.

CONCLUSION

This group provided a sense of community, mutual support, empathic understanding, nonjudgmental treatment of issues, and education. It was hoped that the truth of the participants' inner experiences would have a chance to flourish as they were guided past blocks to awareness. They were able to recognize that they were not alone in their pain and suffering, and that others felt as they did about the molestations. They could express both negative and positive feelings without feeling diminished; they did not have to be ashamed of these emotions. They learned that they could use their power without resorting to force or manipulation, by clearly expressing their needs and setting boundaries. They became more trusting of the intuitive process as the group supported their growth and self-reliance.

BIBLIOGRAPHY

Bass, E., & Davis, L. (1988). *The Courage to Heal; A Guide for Women Survivors of Child Sexual Abuse*. New York: Harper & Row.

Besharov, D. (1990). *Recognizing Child Abuse; The Guide for the Concerned*. New York: Free Press.

Bolton, F. G., Jr. (1989). *Males at Risk*. Newberry Park, CA: Sage Publications.

Buck, J. N. (1970). *The House-Tree-Person Revised Manual*. Los Angeles: Western Psychological Services.

Burgess, A. W., Groth, A. N., Holstrom, L. L., & Sgroi, S. (1978). *Sexual Assault of Children and Adolescents*. Lexington, MA: Lexington Books.

Carozza, P., & Heirsteiner, C. (1983). Young female incest victims in treatment: Stages of growth seen with a group art therapy model. *Clinical Social Work Journal, 10* (3), 165–175.

Chew, J., & Park, K. (1984). *The Secret Game*. Independently distributed.

Dayee, F. (1982). *Private Zone*. New York: Warner Books.

Driver, E., & Droisen, A. (Eds.). (1989) *Child Sexual Abuse: A Feminist Reader*. New York: New York University Press.

Erikson, E. (1950). *Childhood and Society*. New York: W. W. Norton.

Finkelhor, D. (1979). *Sexually Victimized Children*. New York: Free Press.

Forward, S., & Buck, C. (1978). *Betrayal of Innocence: Incest and Its Devastation*. Los Angeles: J. P. Tarcher.

Freeman, L. (1982). *It's My Body*. Seattle: Parenting Press.

Goodwin, J. (1982). *Sexual Abuse: Incest Victims and Their Families*. Boston: John Wright-PSG.

Groth, A. N. (1982). The incest offender. In S. M. Sgroi (Ed.), *Handbook of Clinical Intervention in Child Sexual Abuse* (pp. 215–239). Lexington, MA: Lexington Books.

James, B., & Nasjleti, M. (1983). *Treating Sexually Abused Children and Their Families*. Palo Alto, CA: Consulting Psychologists Press.

Janoff-Bulman, R., & Frieze, I. (1983). A theoretical perspective for understanding reactions to victimization. *Journal of Social Issues, 39*(2), 1–17.

Kramer, E. (1971). *Art as Therapy with Children*. New York: Schocken Books.

Kunzman, K. A. (1990). *Healing Way, Adult Recovery from Sexual Abuse*. San Francisco: Harper & Row.

Landgarten, H. B. (1981). *Clinical Art Therapy: A Comprehensive Guide*. New York: Brunner/Mazel.

Lew, M. (1990). *Victims No Longer: Men Recovering from Incest and Other Sexual Child Abuse*. New York: Harper & Row.

Mayer, M. (1968). *There's a Nightmare in My Closet*. New York: Dial Books.

Naitove, C. (1982). Art therapy with sexually abused children. In S. M. Sgroi (Ed.), *Handbook of Clinical Intervention in Child Sexual Abuse* (pp. 269–308). Lexington, MA: Lexington Books.

Naumburg, M. (1950). *An Introduction to Art Therapy: Studies of the Free Art Expression of Behavior Problem Children and Adolescents as a Means of Diagnosis and Therapy*. New York: Teachers College Press.

Preston, E. (1984). *The Temper Tantrum Book*. Cedar Grove, NJ: Rae.

Rush, F. (1980). *The Best Kept Secret: Sexual Abuse of Children*. Englewood Cliffs, NJ: Prentice-Hall.

Russell, D. (1986). *The Secret Trauma: Incest in the Lives of Girls and Women*. New York: Basic Books.

Sgroi, S. M. (Ed.). (1982). *Handbook of Clinical Intervention in Child Sexual Abuse*. Lexington, MA: Lexington Books.

Stember, C. J. (1980). Art therapy: A new use in the diagnosis and treatment of sexually abused children. In K. McFarlane (Ed.), *Sexual Abuse of Children: Selected Readings* (pp. 59–63). Washington, DC: National Center on Child Abuse and Neglect.

Wadeson, H. (1980). *Art Psychotherapy*. New York: John Wiley.

—6—

Family Art Therapy with Political Refugees

Anne Kellogg and Christine A. Volker

This chapter describes a model of multifamily group therapy used as crisis intervention with a nondiagnosed population of Central American refugees recently arrived in the United States. While this chapter is about a specific population, the model could be adapted to serve groups of families who have experienced uprooting due to homelessness, war, or natural disaster. The process integrates art therapy and group therapy in a supportive environment for the purpose of processing and giving expression to the refugees' journey. The chapter discusses the drawings produced and the dynamics that occurred as a result of the multifamily art therapy. Particular attention is paid to the psychological effects of the uprooting, the migration, and the relocation in the United States.

Before we explain the clinical work, it is important to fully understand the psychological experience of the refugee client. Frelick (1988) defines refugees as, "persons outside their country of origin who are unable or unwilling to return because of persecution, or a well-founded fear of persecution, on the basis of race, religion, nationality, membership in a particular social group or political opinion" (p. 8). A more psychological definition has been given by McEoin (1985), quoting Elie Wiesel: "It is that she or he has no citizenship. Hundreds of thousands, if not millions of human beings, have felt—overnight—unwanted. Now nothing can be more painful than being unwanted, everywhere undesired, and this is what a refugee is" (p. 12). A distinction thus must be made between the immigrant and the refugee. Immigrants move from one country to another voluntarily, usually to improve their economic situation, whereas a refugee leaves a country because of persecution or a fear of persecution.

Approximately a million Central Americans have sought refuge in the United States during the past 10 years to escape the increasing violence and oppression in their own countries. While many of these people received amnesty under the 1986 Immigration Reform and Control Act, hundreds of thousands have illegal status; if returned to their countries of origin, they could be subjected to political reprisals or death. Moreover, many of the families have not arrived in the United States intact. Since, in general, not all family members can migrate at once and some never do get here, families are often fragmented.

The Salvadoran and Guatemalan population discussed in this chapter is made up of four ethnocultural groups: (1) indigenous Indians; (2) blacks and mixed black/Indians; (3) people of European descent, particularly Spanish; and (4) Mestizos and Ladinos, who combine Indian and European ancestry. Nearly all of the Central Americans are Roman Catholic and nearly all have been influenced by the Spanish culture. They speak variations of the Spanish language, Indian dialects, or Creole (Penalosa, 1986).

Almost all of these refugees have experienced the loss of a family member or friend through violence, and many have themselves been tortured. Many have been labeled as "identified criminals" (Aron, 1986) and marked for execution by the death squads. All the refugees who have fled from El Salvador and Guatemala did so for a combination of political and economic reasons. According to Williams and Westermeyer (1986), the most commonly diagnosed psychological problems of Central American refugees are post-traumatic stress disorder, the major mood disorders, and psychosomatic disorders.

The population that is the subject of this discussion was drawn from Casa Rutilio Grande, a sanctuary house serving people from El Salvador and Guatemala. The house provides a temporary refuge for newly arrived refugees who are attempting to integrate their migration and relocation experiences as they adapt to the new culture. They are permitted to stay until they can establish a more stable living situation. All the people living at Casa Rutilio Grande have applied for political asylum.

When the clinical work began, it was hoped that the interventions would provide a therapeutic means by which the families could relive together the conditions of the uprooting, migration, and relocation. The reason for using art therapy was to provide a safe place for the containment and expression of the multiple traumas experienced by the families. It was thought that the art process could facilitate grief and mourning, tap into individual and family strengths, and begin an integration of their past experiences with their present reality. In addition, it was hoped that the artwork would create a document of historical value, substantiating human rights violations and empowering the family in a global context.

ORIENTATION

Before the multifamily art therapy sessions were begun, there was an orientation meeting. Prior to our presenting the proposal to those living and working in the house, we had dinner with everyone and met informally.

We introduced our ideas with the help of a Spanish-speaking interpreter. As we talked, we were met with silence and then, slowly, the questions began. Why, they asked, did we want to help them? How could drawing pictures possibly help? Didn't we realize these issues were better left alone? Tensions were high in the room as the people looked with curiosity, suspicion, and doubt into our Norteamericano faces.

Through our translator, we explained that talking about one's painful experiences can be very difficult, but that expressing oneself through the drawing of these experiences can help get the pain out and provide an opportunity to share with others. We explained that when people keep the pain inside themselves they may hurt even more and that in sharing the experiences they are able to release the pain and support one another. We added that what we learned together during the sessions might help other refugees in their recovery and their entry into this culture.

The basic purpose of this first meeting was to present our proposal to the people and gain their voluntary participation. We attempted to join with the refugees but were met with resistance.

Another meeting was held the next week in order to address the resistance. Present at this meeting were the Central American committee members who administer the house policy, one of the authors, and the Spanish-speaking art therapist who was going to act as facilitator of the sessions. The committee members questioned the therapists, who shared their personal experiences with Central American refugees and their commitment to helping them. The committee members told of their personal experiences and showed graphic pictures of some of the atrocities committed in their countries. The stories told were very emotional and it became clear that all were there for the same reason—to provide a safe, respectful environment for the people to express their feelings and find support. The issue of trust needed to be addressed since the people had come from a climate of fear and distrust in their respective countries. At the close of this meeting, there seemed to be the beginnings of mutual respect, and the committee gave their approval for the project to commence.

GROUP COMPOSITION

The group gathered weekly on a voluntary basis, and the art therapy directives were presented by a bilingual art therapist with Central American background. Both of us were present, with the bilingual art therapist translating for all in attendance. Group size varied, but there were usually 12 to 15 people present each session.

Only two intact families participated. The Estrada family was composed of a mother, Maria-Inez, a father, four sons, Darwin, Daniel, Alberto, and Juanito, ranging in age from 8 to 16, and a male cousin, Alejandro. All but the father, who lived and worked elsewhere in Los Angeles, participated in the sessions. The Chavarras were a reconstituted family consisting of the father, Esteban, the mother, Anna, her two sons, Gustavo, age nine, and René, age seven, and their daughter, Estrelita, age three. Along with these two families from El Salvador were several young men also from El Salvador and two from Guatemala. It is common for one family member to come to the United States ahead of the others in order to establish work and residence.

SESSION 1: THE UPROOTING

Goal:

To establish a safe environment for the people to talk about their experience of uprooting and verbalize their feelings.

Art Directives:

Individuals draw a house, a tree, and a person doing something.

Individuals draw your family doing something together in your country of origin.

This first session introduced the art therapy process and facilitated the beginning of group process. Only a few of the drawings and stories will be discussed.

When we met Anna and Esteban Chavarra at the first session, they were celebrating their marriage, which had taken place two weeks earlier. They had met four years previously in a refugee camp in Honduras, to which Esteban had fled from his village in El Salvador after it was ambushed by government soldiers. The soldiers would often come to the village looking for evidence of guerrilla activity and the villagers would flee, taking with them specially prepared provisions to sustain them in their hiding places until a scout informed them that the soldiers had left.

On one such occasion, the returning villagers were met by a surprise ambush attack and a massacre occurred (documented by Dr. Charley Clements, Amnesty International). Esteban, one of the returning villagers, escaped by diving into a lake and hiding behind a bush. With just his nose and eyes above water, he watched while his village was burned and the inhabitants massacred. He watched while his four children were killed. He watched while soldiers raped his wife and then shot her to death. He watched the soldiers order a young boy to swim to the other side of the lake and dump dead bodies into the water. When the boy said he could not swim, the soldiers threw him into the water and watched him drown.

After the soldiers left, Esteban escaped and found refuge in a refugee camp, where he met Anna who had lost her husband in similar circumstances. Together, they reconstituted a family, migrated to the United States, and found sanctuary at Casa Rutilio Grande. We were able to work with them just three months after their arrival in this country. The artwork of this family during our multifamily sessions depicts the traumas experienced during their uprooting from family, home, and country.

Figure 6.1 shows the family drawing of René Chavarra, age seven. The drawing shows two helicopters flying over his house. One of the helicopters is shooting down and there is a dead person on the ground. One of the trees has fallen over, a symbol that the life force is dying. The use of black on the helicopters and the animals may also signify a sense of death and doom. The Coca-Cola machine is a reminder of American corporate involvement in El Salvador. A lone figure in the foreground confronts the viewer, looking away from the scene. René spoke very directly about his drawing: "Here is the helicopter, here is a dead person, here is a fallen tree." There can be no doubt that the conditions of the uprooting have been traumatic for him. The art process provided him with a graphic means of expressing this trauma.

Esteban's family drawing (Figure 6.2) is especially interesting because he has drawn four children and his wife sitting at a table eating and himself standing in the corner. Esteban explained that he had returned to his village, from the refugee camp in Honduras, to get a table that had been left behind when he fled. He had built the table for his family and retrieving it was important to him. Perhaps it served as his transitional object as he moved from his old life into a new one. A border is drawn encircling the family, symbolically containing the anxiety stirred up by this memory. Esteban explained that the border represented a map of Honduras. He has drawn himself outside the border, looking back at the family. It is interesting to note that in his present family with his new wife, Anna, there are only three

Figure 6.1. René's family drawing.

Figure 6.2. Esteban's family drawing.

Figure 6.3. Juanito's groundless house and person.

Figure 6.4. Juanito's family drawing.

children. Could he have drawn, instead, his family he lost in the massacre in El Salvador?

Figure 6.3 was drawn by Juanito, age eight, the youngest member of the Estrada family. He has drawn a house and a person but no tree. The house and person appear to float in space. There is no baseline or skyline; this lack indicates developmental immaturity, a sign of regression due to his traumatic experiences. The house and person seem isolated and there is an overall feeling of emptiness. Shining above is a mouthless sun with staring eyes, possibly an indicator of his inability to give expression to the trauma. There is a door that appears to be open, a healthy sign indicating emotional access, which was also demonstrated by Juanito's warm interpersonal manner in the session.

In Figure 6.4, Juanito's family drawing, we again see the expressionless, mouthless suns, perhaps indicating that talking about these things is not allowed. The human figures are colored red, looking wounded, which may represent the wounds of the experience. To the far right of the drawing is a head floating upside down without a body. This image may represent an actual observation of a decapitated head, a method of execution reported by refugees. It is interesting to note that the youngest family members' drawings seem the least defended as visual expressions of the experience of uprooting.

During this first session most of the group members participated verbally and shared their pictures with the group. The process was very moving for all of us. Following the session we met with the Spanish-speaking art therapist and went over the drawings, making sure we understood all that had been said.

SESSION 2: THE MIGRATION

Goal:

To provide an experience that gives each person the opportunity to visually and verbally tell the story of his or her journey to the United States.

Art Directive:

Draw together: Make a mural of your journey from your country of origin to the United States showing what happened along the way.

At the second session the people gathered around the table, which had been covered with a long sheet of butcher paper. They were asked to draw the experiences of their journey to the United States.

Figure 6.5 is René's mural scene depicting the weapons of war: black helicopters flying overhead shooting bullets while two figures, one with a machine gun, stand below. A black house is drawn, possibly suggesting depression, and a tree is drawn inside a mountain of little trees that has been watercolored in such a way as to suggest bleeding. A smiling sun shines down upon the scene, an ever-present symbol of hope, or perhaps denial.

Figure 6.6 tells the story of two Estrada brothers crossing a river on their way from El Salvador through Guatemala to Mexico. Their art is more sophisticated, revealing their familiarity with drawing. They drew a jungle forest of trees on the Guatemalan side of the river. The trees are drawn with heavy green lines, perhaps indicating danger or anxiety. A military man with a gun is demanding money from one person; another person, drawn in gray, is lying on the ground. The fallen figure would seem to indicate death at the hands of the military man. Meanwhile, several figures on rafts are being escorted across the river by swimmers. Once in Mexico, on the other side of the river, two figures are seen walking into the trees, which are drawn in a much less anxious style. This could indicate a feeling of being safe once in Mexico.

Paco, a staff person at Casa Rutilio Grande for six months, who has been in the United States for three years, is dedicated to helping those who arrive from his country. He took part in only a few sessions. In Figure 6.7, he illustrated his journey by showing how the military arrested him for being a student. He explained that students were viewed as subversives. Paco was arrested and put in Mariona Prison in El Salvador. His experience of torture with electric shock was still too terrible for him to talk about. He drew the graveyard outside the prison where many dead prisoners, less fortunate than he, lay buried.

We do not know how Paco escaped this prison. He has drawn the barbed-wire fence at the border of Mexico and the United States, and the Immigration Border Patrol man carrying the gun. Paco reported that it was at this point in his journey that he proclaimed, "If I am going to die, then I want to do it on Latin soil." He continued his story by stating that, when he first arrived in Los Angeles, he spent his nights sleeping in an inner-city park until coming to Casa Grande.

Paco's story was painful to hear. He had been in the United States much longer than most of the people in the group and he appeared to be in less denial. He seemed to have readier access to his feelings of loss, grief, and anger. Clearly, the conditions of his uprooting are still being integrated with his journey and current relocation.

The refugees' stories of their individual journeys were very powerful and seemed to add to the group's cohesiveness. While each story was different, the drawing of their experiences on one piece of paper suggested a connected-

Figure 6.5. René's weapons of war.

Figure 6.6. The journey of two brothers.

Figure 6.7. Paco's escape from the Mariona prison.

ness and a common bond in their uprooting and migration. The session was very emotional for all present.

SESSION 3: THE RELOCATION

Goal:

To provide an experience that allows each person the opportunity to express his or her feelings about life in the United States.

Art Directives:

Draw separately: Draw family doing something together in this country.

Collage: Choose some pictures that describe your feelings about your life in the United States. Cut them out and glue them down on a piece of paper.

In the third multifamily session, two directives were given to the group for the purpose of assessing the relocation experience. The first directive was individually to draw their families doing something together in this country. Felt pens were the only materials provided. The predominant images were of the church, Casa Grande, the city streets and freeways, the Casa Grande van, and scenes of helping others and searching for work. The need for work, coupled with a fear of being arrested by the immigration officials, pervaded the drawings of the adults. There was a somber, depressed atmosphere as each adult reported his or her difficulty in finding work. Some reported leaving the house before dawn to look for a job and returning after dark, discouraged by the lack of work. Those who did find work received wages far below the legal minimum wage.

The artwork supports the research by Penalosa (1986) that shows that work is the primary need for those who arrive here from Central America.

Ten out of 14 drawings are monochromatic, which may indicate depression. Of these 10, four have one or more details of yellow (sun, moon, headlights), which appear to be indicators of hope. Two of these showed helicopters, and in one picture, Figure 6.8, by René, the helicopter is shooting a figure holding a machine gun pointed upwards outside Casa Grande. A number of people are inside the house, sitting at a table, and two figures stand at the entrance. The outline of the house seems to provide a safe containment for the people. Outside the entrance, another figure in black holds a machine gun; however, the image has been scribbled out.

The recurring theme of the shooting helicopter is seen in many of the children's drawings and seems to symbolize a common trauma of war they have experienced in their country. The children are also aware of helicopters

Figure 6.8. Life at Casa Grande.

in the skies over Los Angeles; many evenings a helicopter can be heard flying over Casa Grande. For René, the black image of the shooting helicopter represents a threat not only from the past, but in the present. This is an example of the intrusion of thoughts and feelings associated with past trauma, which is one of the diagnostic symptoms of the post-traumatic stress disorder.

Five of the pictures portray people on the streets looking for work, as illustrated by Maria-Inez Estrada in Figure 6.9. This monochromatic picture is drawn with the repetitive images of despair and the words: ''Sin trabajo'' (without work), and ''Tienes permiso'' (Do you have permission to work?), and ''Busco trabajo'' (I am searching for work).

The second directive given at the session was to choose some magazine pictures that describe feelings about life in the United States, and make a collage. While the first directive seemed to elicit a depressed affect, the second had the opposite effect. There was much laughter as the people went through the pictures and joked about the ''beautiful women.'' Most people cut out their shapes very carefully and, after gluing them to the paper, wrote down some words to describe them.

There were images of beautiful women, fancy houses, cars, and Disneyland. There were a variety of responses that told what each person did or

Sin Trabajo

tienes permiso
busco Trabajo

Figure 6.9. Looking for work.

did not like about the United States. Señora Estrada (the mother of the intact family), whose viewpoint about the United States in the previous session had been quite negative, seemed to focus on the positive aspects of her stay. Her central theme in Figure 6.10 was illustrated by an image of a woman holding her head in her hands and saying that she is "preoccupied with many things." Around this face were many positive pictures about the United States, with such captions as: "Here my daughters can study and have opportunity in the future" and "Here there is freedom of expression." There was a large white baby hand under the thoughtful woman and several other images saying, "There are persons here with good hearts," "They give me a hand," and "The children come with happy faces." The hands in the collage all seemed to be expressions of the care and hospitality experienced by this woman in the United States.

The first directive had helped us get in touch with the despair experienced by the refugees in their search for work. Their response to the second directive showed their hope that they would find new opportunities in the United States. The evening seemed to end on a happy note, with much laughter about the magazine images and expectation for a better life in this country.

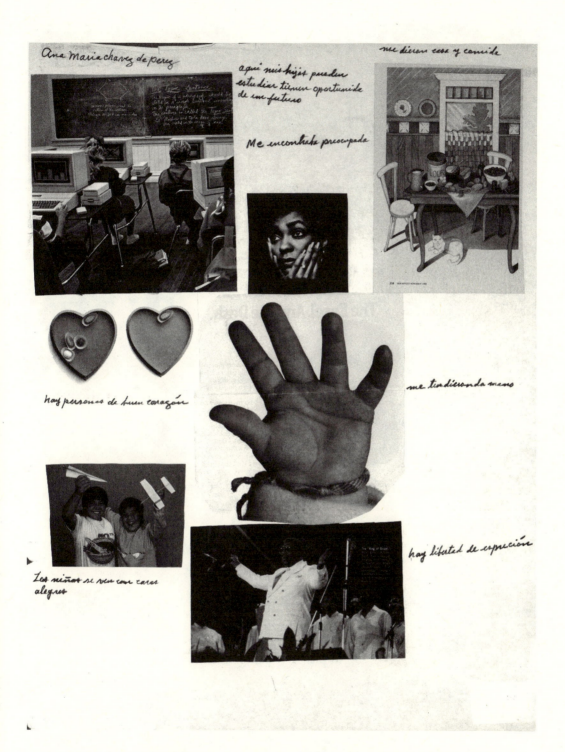

Figure 6.10. Impressions of the United States.

Figure 6.11. Memories of El Salvador.

Figure 6.12. Leaving one's country behind.

SESSION 4: INTEGRATION

Goal:

To provide each individual with an art experience that integrates the past migration with the present relocation.

Art Directive:

Draw yourself in your family before the journey and draw yourself in your family now.

The fourth session was designed to provide an opportunity for integration. Responding to the art directive, Esteban Chavarra chose four images to represent his country of origin, El Salvador. He did not include the relocation experience, which may indicate his struggle in accepting his new residence. Figure 6.11 shows these four images: (1) two men riding horses, which he said signified life in the country; (2) a scene of the desert, which he said represented the crisis in El Salvador; (3) an old woman and her granddaughter, which he said symbolized love and respect for the elderly; and (4) a perspiring brown boy with a thermometer in his mouth, representing the sick ones. As he shared his pictures, he told of the crisis in El Salvador; of the war, the hunger, and the illness.

While the directive had been to draw, the children all used collage to represent the United States. They used felt pens and chalk to draw their country of origin. In Figure 6.12, René chose pictures of white people in

beautiful settings to represent the culture he had entered. He drew Casa Grande as part of his scene of El Salvador with the Casa Grande van connecting both past and present. This illustrates how Casa Grande had become a sanctuary and a refuge of his country within this country, a microcosm of his culture relocated in the larger culture of Los Angeles. While the people he drew are faceless, for the first time he drew a sun with a mouth and nose. High in the sky he placed a cut-out image of the world, like a bridge between the two cultures. This is the same child who had repeatedly drawn the helicopter shooting from the sky. As part of an intact family, he probably has a better chance of making a healthy adjustment to the relocation (Garcia, 1988).

The three-year-old girl, Estrelita, used glue, pen, masking tape, and collage as she experimented in a developmentally appropriate way, creating Figure 6.13. When asked to share her ideas, she called her artwork ''La bomba.'' Both she and the two young boys were the only ones who mentioned bombs. The adults did not respond to this or talk about it. The children seemed to have more direct access to their memories of the trauma of the war. The adults seldom referred directly to the conditions of the war or the uprooting.

Thus far, the sessions were structured to provide a sequential opportunity for expression and integration of the many traumas these people had experienced. Session 1 facilitated the creation of a symbol to represent the memory

Figure 6.13. ''La bomba.''

of their lives in their homeland. Session 2 allowed for the representation of the struggles of the migration, and session 3 for the creation of an image to represent their present reality in the United States.

Many of the people, particularly the children, made their collage about their relocation on one sheet of paper and their drawing about their homeland on another piece. At some point in the session the children began taping their two drawings together with masking tape. This process of connecting the pictures provided a means of symbolically integrating the migration and the relocation. We were impressed at the way the process happened so naturally.

SESSION 5: STRENGTHS

Goal:

To increase each person's awareness of his or her personal strengths both before the uprooting and as a result of the migration and relocation.

Art Directive:

Make a symbol to represent your own personal strength and place it in the middle of the table when finished.

The purpose of the fifth session was to assist the people, through the art, in accessing their personal strengths developed as a result of their migrating to the United States. By getting in touch with their inner resources, each person, it is hoped, would be able to utilize these in their present situation. Colored plasticene was used for the creating of the symbol. The people in the group seemed to enjoy this new material, laughing and playing with it. Most people made more than one art piece to represent their strengths. The ability to endure hardship and keep going, as well as their faith, seemed to be strengths that were common to all. One man made a heart and cross, saying that his strength was "his love and his faith," while another man made a red cup representing "the blood of Christ," which was his source of strength (Figure 6.14)

Each person placed his or her symbol in the center of the table while speaking of his or her strengths. The sharing and discussion seemed to reinforce these strengths and build self-esteem.

Figure 6.14. "The blood of Christ."

SESSION 6: CELEBRATION

Goal:

To provide a ritual to celebrate the bonding and sense of community that had developed as a result of sharing their experiences of uprooting, migration, and relocation.

Art Directive:

Paint a banner together to celebrate your community's strength at Casa Grande.

The final session of the project was designed to celebrate the refugees' experience together and the sense of community developed as a result of the multifamily group art therapy. Cloth, fabric paints, and brushes were provided for the making of the large banner together. There were many symbols of strength and happiness: hearts, flags, suns, trees, flowers, stars, birds, and eggs. Many wrote words of love and peace, as well as their own names and the name of their country.

Everyone participated enthusiastically, with older members helping younger ones. We also joined in the painting of the banner, wanting to share in the process of celebration and to express our solidarity with the people of Casa Grande.

Following the completion of the banner, the group adjourned to the meeting room upstairs to evaluate the art sessions and give feedback about the process. The consensus of the community was overwhelming in its support of the project.

The banner remained in the house, providing the group and groups to come with a reminder of the cohesion that had developed as a result of the process. It is a symbol that celebrates their community together and our involvement with them.

DISCUSSION

From individual statements presented at the evaluation meeting, it was apparent that the art therapy process, more than any other form of therapy that had previously been used at Casa Grande, contributed to the integration of the participants' past experience with their present reality, and to their transition into this culture. In addition, the visual imagery helped them to get in touch with painful past events that may have taken much longer in verbal therapy owing to their defense mechanisms. They told us that this was not easy, but it was necessary. Because the visual imagery cuts through defenses so quickly, it is essential for clinicians to recognize the importance of not always interpreting the material.

In retrospect, it is valuable to acknowledge and discuss the reccurring symbols that were evident in the art produced throughout the six sessions of this multifamily group. The imagery often expressed concern with disappearances. Figures that became faint and seemed to disappear were frequent, as were running persons apparently portraying the theme of leaving the country. The images may also indicate fear of being "disappeared" by death squads or fear connected with the necessity to flee. Perhaps the images suggest the loved ones left behind who are fading away in memory.

Another repeated theme is the uprooted tree. Burns (1987) writes, "Perhaps the most frequent and universal metaphor depicting human development is the tree." With this in mind, the symbol of the uprooted tree may depict the uprootedness of these people. There are also many images of heavily laden fruit trees, which may symbolize a preoccupation with food and nurturance.

One of the most predominant themes running through the children's drawings is that showing the destructive weapons of warfare—the helicopters firing down, the man with the machine gun, and the bomb. These represent the intrusion into their present reality of the traumas of war.

The floating houses found in many of the pictures seem to symbolize the reality that these people do not presently have a home. They have left their homes behind and Casa Grande is only a temporary respite. These floating houses, without any baseline and often without a door, symbolize the insecure existence of a refugee who is homeless in a foreign country. They represent the person who does not feel as if he or she belongs anywhere.

The floating house, the uprooted tree, and the running man all symbolize the trauma of the uprooting, the migration, and the relocation.

The creation of symbols to explore the uprooting, the migration, and the relocation offered the people an opportunity to address the traumas and to integrate them into the present. The art process seemed to provide a bridge to aid in the transition from their war-torn homelands to their present life in Los Angeles.

For many reasons, the art process seemed to offer these families a different kind of opportunity to deal with their experiences as refugees. In part, this was because the art was generationally leveling, allowing everyone to participate at their own developmental stage. The children seemed to find the process most comfortable. The older the individuals were, the stronger their defense mechanisms had become and the more defended the art appeared.

Casa Grande and the art therapy group it offered provided a sanctuary, a refuge for those people from Central America who had suffered many traumas in their own country, on their journey to this country, in the crossing of several borders, and in their attempts to survive in the United States. McEoin (1985) included an essay by David Napier that eloquently defines sanctuary:

> We know that it [sanctuary] is more than a place. We believe sanctuary is a series of related acts, or even gestures of healing, in a context of incomprehensible monumental wounds in the corporate body and flesh and mind and spirit of countries and barrios, human communities and families—especially for us now, in Central America.

For us, this project was only a "gesture of healing" in the context of "incomprehensible wounds." The brief crisis intervention work did not allow for addressing the many losses in any depth. During our work at Casa Grande, we have come to admire and respect the strength and courage of the men, women, and children whom we met. Through the art process and product, we hope we validated this strength and normalized the natural responses that come from going through such out-of-the-ordinary experiences. We attempted to normalize these feelings and to facilitate containment of the pain in the context of the art.

CONCLUSION

Casa Grande is only a stopping point in the continuing journey of the recently arrived refugees. Most of them spend a month in the house before going on to another location. It is a place to rest and a place in which to collect oneself following the migration. Casa Grande creates a community out of the families and fragments of families that arrive. The art therapy was able to contribute to the bonding of these people during their short stay, as they shared their experiences through visual images. Their participation in a group with people who had gone through similar traumas helped to normalize this experience. The process helped to open them up to each other. This was a necessary step in their healing. We were told that they may give testimonies in the community at large, but they seldom talk with each other about the past. Many have needed to defend themselves psychologically in order to deal with the present circumstances and to continue the journey.

This model of multifamily art therapy could be used with any group of families that have experienced a common trauma. Families may experience uprooting, migration, and relocation due to natural disaster, homelessness, and war. Multifamily art therapy for nondiagnosed populations might be effectively used both as crisis intervention and to head off and cope with later psychological problems.

BIBLIOGRAPHY

Acosta, A., & Domino, G. (1987). The relation of acculturation and values in Mexican-Americans. *Hispanic Journal of Behavioral Sciences, 9*(2).

Albert, M., Cagan, L., Chomsky, N., Hahnel, R., King, M., Sargent, L., & Sklar, H. (1986). *Liberating Theory*. Boston: South End Press.

Amaro, H. (1988). Women in the Mexican-American community: Religion, culture and the reproductive attitudes and experiences. *Journal of Community Psychology, 16*(1), 7–21.

Argueta, M. (1983). *One Day of Life*. New York: Vintage.

Aron, A. (1986). *Psychological problems of Salvadoran refugees in California*. Paper presented at the American Psychological Association, Washington, DC.

Bettelheim, B. (1980). *Surviving*. New York: Vintage.

Burns, R. (1982). *Self-growth in Families: Kinetic Family Drawings, Research and Application*. New York: Brunner/Mazel.

Burns, R. (1987). *Kinetic House-Tree-Person Drawings: An Interpretative Manual*. New York: Brunner/Mazel.

Cervantes, R., Salgado, S., Nelly, V., & Padilla, A. (1988). *Post-Traumatic Stress Disorder Among Immigrants from Central America and Mexico*. Spanish Speaking Mental Health Research Center, Occasional Paper No.

Chomsky, N. (1988). *The Culture of Terrorism*. Boston: South End Press.

Cienfuegos, A., & Monelli, C. (1983). The testimony of political repression as a therapeutic instrument. *American Journal of Orthopsychiatry, 53*(1), 43–51.

Dilling, Y., & Rogers, I. (1984). *In Search of Meaning.* Scottdale, PA: Herald Press.

Frelick, B. (1988, Nov.). An open door for some. *Sojourners*, 8–9.

Garcia, S. (1988). *Families who have suffered trauma due to migration* (Cassette Recording No. 4). Child Abuse Association.

Golub, D. (1981). Symbolic expression in post-traumatic stress disorder. *Arts in Psychotherapy, 8.*

Grossman, F. (1981). Creativity as a means of coping with anxiety. *Arts in Psychotherapy, 8*, 185–192.

Kinzie, J., & Fleck, J. (1987). Psychotherapy with severely traumatized refugees. *American Journal of Psychotherapy, 41*, 83–94.

Lofgren, D. (1981). Art therapy and cultural differences. *American Journal of Art Therapy, 21*, 25–30.

Manz, B. (1985). *Refugees of a Hidden War.* New York: State University of New York Press.

McEoin, G. (1985). *Sanctuary.* San Francisco: Harper & Row.

McGoldrick, M., Pearce, J., & Giordana, J. (1982). *Ethnicity and Family Therapy.* New York: Guilford Press.

Penalosa, F. (1986). *Central Americans in Los Angeles: Background, Language, Education.* Spanish Speaking Mental Health Research Center, Occasional Paper No. 21.

Randall, M. (1985). *Women Brave in the Face of Danger.* New York: The Crossing Press.

Rubenstein, R. (1975). *The Cunning of History.* New York: Harper & Row.

Trejo, A. (Ed.). (1980). *The Chicanos, as We See Ourselves.* Tucson: University of Arizona Press.

Williams, C., & Westermeyer, J. (Eds.). (1986). *Refugee Mental Health in Resettlement Countries.* Washington, DC: Hemisphere.

— SECTION III —

FORMULATING ANSWERS

−7−

Family Systems and the Creative Process: The Second Look

Debra Linesch

Chapters 2 through 6 have provided clinical illustrations for the main concept of this book—that the psychotherapeutically directed art process can uniquely and effectively meet the needs of families in serious psychological disorder.

Although the scenarios described in the case examples provide, in themselves, the richest access to an understanding of the relationship between the art process and family change, I developed a three-question framework to identify and analyze consistencies between the diverse case materials. This conceptual framework served to simplify the family art experience so that three main ideas emerged: (1) that the art process facilitated members' affective self-expression; (2) that the art process encouraged genuine communication between family members; and (3) that the art process helped empower family members to acknowledge, take responsibility for, and hopefully modify their roles within the family system. Following is a summary of the simple concepts that were delineated.

RELEASE AND RELIEF

When encouragement to participate in the art process was offered to individuals immersed in complicated and chaotic family systems, the consequent self-expression helped relieve the pressures, serving as a preliminary and necessary step in the complex process of systemic change.

In Chapter 2 the clinical material illustrated the manner in which the art process was able to quickly expose the underlying dynamics of family crises. Behavior patterns and communication styles were able to surface as the family collaboratively created systemic metaphors. These graphic displays of the ways in which the family members interacted during crises provided the distressed systems with an alternate form of communication. Both intrapsychic and interpsychic processes were able to be pictorially represented. Through the art, the family members found ways to release, relieve, and reconstruct the experiences that had become both causes and symptoms of the crisis.

Chapter 3 demonstrated how the emotional burdens and burnout of the single parent were relieved when involvement in the art process was offered. When these mothers were provided with the opportunity to create symbols of their internal experiences within a context where the latent meanings of these productions were understood, they felt affirmed. Since the art process offered all the members of the single-parent families the opportunity for self-expression, it offered the mothers new vantage points from which to observe and understand their families. For these families, becoming involved in creative projects can be likened to finding a safety valve through which to release the pressure. As a result of this, the subsequent calm and sense of relief fulfilled the necessary conditions for the family to be reached psychotherapeutically.

In Chapter 4 the art process was explored in terms of its efficacy to elicit the unconscious material often observed in the interfamilial dynamics of alcohol abuse. The artwork produced by the entire family system and individually by its members offered a substantial opportunity for the expression of alcoholism. Authentically created representations of the intrapsychic and interpsychic experiences of alcohol abuse temporarily freed the clients from their habitual and redundant patterns of behavior. The symptomatic interactions, now available throughout the arts' metaphors, provided new starting points from which psychotherapeutic gains for the entire family could be made.

Chapter 5 described the important role the art process plays in penetrating the system-sanctioned denial against acknowledging or "feeling" incestuous sexual abuse. Once again, the art productions offered metaphorical opportunities for the expression of material that the family system had "decided" were secrets. The artistically created symbols became signifiers of the pain, the anger, the guilt, and the fear that tend to paralyze the incestuous family system. Provided with this symbolic pathway for expression, both the abused children and their parents were able to experience some relief and a consequent augmentation of accessibility to systemic interventions.

In Chapter 6 the authors discussed the manner in which the art process helped families traumatized by war, poverty, and migration express and make use of their personal histories. In many cases, these histories were characterized by inhuman travesties and incomprehensible suffering. The individuals and families who had lived through and survived became themselves the containers for the intolerable, untellable experiences. The art process provided opportunities (alternate pathways for the verbally blocked material) of relief.

Although the populations discussed in the five chapters are diverse, their common link is family-system disruption. The art process offered its first healing step in providing opportunities for the expression of the often horrific internal experiences maintained and denied by the individuals within the family system.

EXPRESSION AND DIALOGUE

The art process offered a second healing step for the members of these disrupted families. Throughout the clinical material, it is possible to observe the manner in which the art facilitated interfamilial dialogue. Communication grew out of self-expression and family members were able to share experiences, feelings, and hopes in ways that were freed of rigid systemic limitations.

In Chapter 2 the clinical material illustrated how the art process strengthened the trauma-impacted dialogue between members of families experiencing severe crises. Throughout the examples, all the family members had individually experienced the crises as isolating and distancing. While they were able to make use of the art's power to facilitate self-expression, they were simultaneously able to enter into new kinds of dialogical relationships with other family members. The metaphorical representations of the suffering family system helped the family members listen to each other and hear each other's experiences. In this way, their isolation was decreased and individuals were able to experience members of their families as struggling but empathic colleagues in the entire system's process of crisis resolution.

Chapter 3 presented useful examples that demonstrate how the concrete symbolic process augments interfamilial communication that has been strained by the dynamics of single parenthood. The art experience provided both the single mothers and their children with opportunities to hear and be heard, and then to respond to each other. The overburdened, exhausted, and depleted single mothers made use of the metaphoric potential in creative expression in two important ways—attending to their children more and more on a feeling level while simultaneously reinforcing their own limit-setting attempts. The reciprocally strengthening dialogue that can be helpful to the faltering single-parent family system was facilitated by the immediacy of the images the mothers and children created.

In Chapter 4 the alcoholic family was discussed and the art process was demonstrated as a useful tool to support the family members' faltering efforts to genuinely address each other and overcome the characteristic denial. In alcoholic family systems, years of mutually agreed-upon denial can make system intervention inordinately difficult. In art therapy, families that have developed redundant verbal patterns that support systemic denial can approach and experience more authentic dialogue through the art process. The graphic exchanges shift the family outside their natural communication mode, thereby offering them the opportunity to say new things to each other in new ways and to hear new things from each other in new ways. In the case example presented in the chapter, mother and son benefited enormously from the experience of drawing together, creating a metaphorical dialogue that inevitably focused on issues of separation and independence.

Chapter 5 described an intervention model that utilizes the art process to help families that have experienced the ravages of incestuous sexual abuse to increase intergenerational interactions. Once the family members experienced a sense of relief provided by the self-expressive potential of the art process, they were able to engage in increasingly meaningful dialogue. The chapter clearly identified the way in which intergenerational empathy was facilitated by the powerful imagery that emerged in the sexually abused girls' drawings. As the children moved closer and closer to graphically documenting their pain and fear, the mothers were accordingly engaged in the children's affective life.

In Chapter 6 the art process, as used by recently migrated Central American refugees, was discussed in terms of its potential to facilitate genuine communication about the members' denied but shared personal histories. This kind of authentic artistic communication created the foundations for dialogue between individuals who shared tragic backgrounds. This dialogue was necessary to support what the authors of this chapter described as their "gesture of healing."

In all five chapters, the art experience provided a vehicle for the individuals to take advantage of increased self-expressive abilities and share their internal experiences as communication between family/system members.

THE OPPORTUNITY FOR CHANGE

The art process was effective in supporting the family systems' utilization of the members' increased self-expression and expanded dialogue in order to create systemic change.

Chapter 2 discussed the manner in which the art directives aided the therapist's attempts to empower family members and strengthened roles diminished by severe crises. With both the families discussed, the art process facilitated the negotiation of shifts within the family structures. In the first family, the mother used the art to experiment in new ways with parental assertion; in the second family, the father's experience of his daughter's artwork empowered him to relieve her of her parentified role. Roles that had been rigidified by the crises the families were experiencing were opened up for exploration, evaluation, and change by the dialogue created in the art process.

Chapter 3 discussed clinical material that clearly demonstrated the efficacy of the art process in establishing generational boundaries and empowering appropriate roles in single-parent families. As children were able to communicate their developmental needs very clearly in the art process, the mothers were able to increasingly experience their children with more clarity. At the same time, the role and boundary ambiguity that frequently occurs in the single-parent family became available for observation in the metaphors that emerged artistically. As this ambiguity grew apparent, structural interventions by the art therapist were successful in helping the families redefine roles and boundaries in ways that were more appropriate and helpful for both mothers and children.

In Chapter 4 the case material presented the art process as a powerful tool in clarifying and providing opportunity for amendments of family roles distorted by the pervasive effects of alcoholism. Although the clinical example discussed in the chapter does not demonstrate the ways in which the art process actually helped to empower the family members to make changes in their habitual patterns, it does illustrate the potential for that to happen. Increasingly authentic self-expression coupled with increasingly open inter-familial communication supports the kinds of risk-taking and experimentation that are required for behavioral changes within the family system. It is quite possible to speculate that if the family had continued their metaphorical expressions, the systemic consequences of father's alcoholism would have been augmented in exposure, acknowledgment, and dialogue. Ultimately, this augmentation acts to counteract the denial that frequently is an obstacle to change within the alcoholic family system.

Chapter 5 discussed a model of treatment intervention in which the art process was effective in positively restructuring families destroyed by incestuous sexual abuse. The clinical examples of this chapter illustrate the manner in which the expressive communication (facilitated by the art process) strengthened behavioral and systemic changes. As the victims of the incestuous abuse (both daughters and mothers) released and shared their stories, metaphorically and directly, they were increasingly freed of shame, humiliation, and guilt. Consequently, they were empowered in their abilities to express their needs and set limits, indeed to make major structural changes to the systems in which the abuse had occurred.

In Chapter 6 the case material demonstrated how the art process rejuvenated Central American refugee families and enabled them to find strength from their personal histories so as to advance the process of assimilation. As the authors of this chapter so poignantly described, the art experience seemed to offer the families involved in the multifamily art therapy group the opportunity to integrate their experience of relocation. Their self-expression, enriched by the art process, and their communication, facilitated by the art process, metaphorically enabled the refugees to create transitions between their war-torn past and the challenges of the present.

In all five chapters, the art process catalyzed, supported, or provided vehicles for systemic change. The changes experienced by the family systems were, in each case, a complex consequence of three steps: enriched personal self-expression, increasingly authentic interpersonal communication, and individual empowerment as the final step that could never have occurred without the first two steps. The art process, in its power to create imagery and metaphors, allows for the emergence of patterns and processes deep within personal and interpersonal lives.

SYNTHESIS

The families discussed in this book all experienced tremendous amounts of conflict, disorganization, and pain. The types of distress they experienced and the consequent systemic defenses they manifested can become obstacles to psychotherapeutic intervention. I believe that this book has demonstrated that the integration of the art process with family therapy interventions can minimize such defensive obstacles. The creative and symbolic power of the art process is based on the interrelatedness between self-expression, genuine dialogue, and role empowerment. When this interrelatedness is understood and utilized for psychotherapeutic growth, the full potential of family art therapy is made available.

Index